Why We Love
the People We Do
& How They Sometimes
Drive Us Crazy

ALSO BY DAPHNE ROSE KINGMA

True Love
*How to Make Your Relationship
Sweeter, Deeper, and More Passionate*

Finding True Love
*The Four Essential Keys to
Discovering the Love of Your Life*

Heart & Soul
Living the Joy, Truth & Beauty of Your Intimate Relationship

The Future of Love
The Power of the Soul in Intimate Relationships

The Men We Never Knew
How to Deepen Your Relationship with the Man You Love

Weddings from the Heart
*Contemporary and Traditional Ceremonies
for an Unforgettable Wedding*

A Garland of Love
Daily Reflections on the Magic and Meaning of Love

Coming Apart
*Why Relationships End and
How to Live Through the Ending of Yours*

Why We Love
the People We Do

& How They Sometimes
Drive Us Crazy

(also published as *The 9 Types of Lovers*)

Daphne Rose Kingma

MJF BOOKS
NEW YORK

Published by MJF Books
Fine Communications
Two Lincoln Square
60 West 66th Street
New York, NY 10023

Why We Love the People We Do and How They Sometimes Drive Us Crazy
Library of Congress Control Number 00-135238
ISBN 1-56731-423-6

Manufactured in the United States of America on acid-free paper

MJF Books and the MJF colophon are trademarks of Fine Creative Media, Inc.

10   9   8   7   6   5   4   3   2

For Molly
who inspired it

I. L. Y.

Why We Love
the People We Do
& How They Sometimes
Drive Us Crazy

ACKNOWLEDGMENTS

Loving thanks to the hands and hearts
who held my hand and heart
throughout the writing of this book.

To Yeshe Pema, for feeding me and making me home,
 and to Suntah for bringing us together.
To Patricia Mary Rose Robertson,
 for healing, prayers, and nurturing.
To Arthur, for sacred witness.
To Dave, for seeing me through.
To Laura, for steadfastness.
To "Sarita," for always being "awn it."
To my dear sister, Chris, for abiding.
To Al and Marianne for being there still.
To Will Glennon, for constancy and love.

To my editor, Mary Jane Ryan, for once again,
and so beautifully, bringing it all together.
To Don and Ana Li,
who gave us space and grace in the process.
And much love to Molly, who's been there all along.

LOVE TYPES

What Really Drives
Our Intimate Relationships

This book is a tool for discovery on your journey to love, whether you'd like to find a person with whom to have a satisfying relationship or just make your current relationship more enjoyable.

I strongly believe that in this life, love is the only journey worth taking. It's through falling in love and living our intimate personal relationships that we have the pleasure of getting to know another person, sharing our life experiences, and having the emotional, sexual, and just plain day-to-day companionship that doubles our joys and halves our sorrows. Love is the richest treasure of being human.

If you would like to have a wonderful relationship but haven't been able to create one, or if in the relationship you do have you seem to be dogged by repetitive complaints or issues that never quite resolve, it may be because you don't have a clear understanding of your own or your partner's personality type, or of how your two types are interacting.

I've written this book because I love to teach people about how to love. I've spent my professional life, both in my counseling practice and through a number of books, helping people learn to love better by teaching about the attitudes, skills, and practices that are the essential components of being a loving human being. I've written about how to end a relationship and go through the emotional process of parting, how to develop the specific skills of loving, how to better understand the man you love, how to take your relationship to a spiritual level, and even how our world of relationships as a whole is moving toward the spiritual.

Recently, however, I have come to see that while it's all well and good to have high hopes, even spiritual ideals, for your relationship, if you don't know some of the basics— who you are as a personality, for example, and what makes you and your partner tick—your relationships still won't work as well as they might. In short, it doesn't matter how lofty your ideals are—all the skills and attitudes in the world won't work unless you also understand your own personality type and your partner's and how they operate in a relationship.

That's because while each of us is a unique and unrepeatable human being with particular personality characteristics and a spiritual essence, we each also fall into one of nine basic personality types that deeply affect the way we relate to others. And since, on the emotional level, it is our personality types, above all, that dictate how we react in relationships, unless you understand your love type and your partner's, you'll continue to be frustrated and confused in your relationships. The person you love will keep on behaving in ways that irritate and baffle you. And you'll keep behaving in ways that drive him or her a little crazy.

That's why, after everything else I've taught, I'm now turning my attention to the impact of personality types on our intimate relationships—so you can have a basic map of what's going on with you and your partner, and you can love each other better.

I remember counseling one couple over a period of several years. Every time they came into my office, they were at each other's throats about one thing or another. Although each session we'd work through a given problem, every time they came back, they'd show up with another problem, and more frustration.

Finally, one day in exasperation, I said to them, "Don't you two ever have any fun?!" "Oh, yes," they both chimed in at once. "Most of the time we have a wonderful time. It's just that we have a bundle of issues that keep coming up in one form or another and when we're here, we don't need to talk about how great things are; we need to talk about our problems." "He always treats everything as if it's no big deal," said the woman. "And she always overreacts to everything," said the man.

Like most of the rest of us, this couple had a recurring set of relationship problems. These problems existed not because they had a bad relationship or because they didn't love each other, but because of the way their two different personality types interacted. Their repetitive problems revealed what most of us experience in relationships: conflicts created by the interaction of two types of personalities who each approach life—and the relationship itself—in a very different way. Because this is true, the more we understand and appreciate these differences, the more harmonious and happy our relationships can be.

You and Your Personality

Every human being has a personality that is pretty readily distinguishable and reveals a great deal about each of us. The specifics of your own personality may be so ingrained and familiar that you almost can't see them at all. Nevertheless, your personality traits control to a great extent what you like and dislike, how you respond to life's events, and, above all, how you love.

Our personalities are the result of the interaction of our innate temperament—the traits we inherited from our parents—with the vast collection of all the experiences we have in life. They are made up of the whole constellation of external behaviors and internal feelings that each of us develops in response to life situations. Personality is each person's unique and natural way of reacting to life and interacting in the world. In a very real way, our personalities *are* us.

Our personalities are especially affected by our childhood experiences—for example, the houses we lived in, the way our parents treated each other and us, the number of our siblings and where we're located in that lineup—and above all by what I call our "life issues." A life issue is the central emotional wound that each of us experienced, as well as all the behaviors we've developed to cope with, compensate for, avoid, or overcome the painful emotional charge of that wound.

4 ∎

Because our wounds and coping mechanisms are formed through exposure to common life experiences, such as abandonment, emotional abuse or neglect, serious illness, betrayal, or the death of a parent, it turns out that there is only a limited number of basic types of personalities. That is, there are a number of predictable ways human beings respond to particular emotional events, and it is this constellation of typical responses that forms the core of a given personality type.

As you read through the descriptions of the nine personality types in this book, you will come to see both the chief emotional wound and the coping mechanisms of each type, and, as a consequence, the way each type tends to operate in intimate relationships.

Personality Types in Love

Over the years there have been a number of systems of personality types. The famous psychologist Carl Jung created a very elaborate system. There's also a system called the Enneagram, which defines a number of types and sub-types of personality, as well as the Myers-Briggs personality analysis, which divides people into sixteen highly differentiated types.

The personality types we will be exploring here are not based on any of these systems. Rather, they are based on my observation of thousands of people in relationships and more than twenty-five years of clinical practice in helping them understand themselves and their partners.

In this system, there are nine prominent love types, each with particular distinguishing characteristics. These types are a little like various other categories we use to describe ourselves. Just as blondes, brunettes, redheads, and people with raven-black hair are all human beings, they are nevertheless distinguishable from one another by their hair color. We are also distinguished from one another by the color of our eyes, our general body types, our blood types, and our nationalities.

So it is with personality. While we all have this psychological quality called personality, and for each of us it is unique, there are nevertheless some predominating characteristics that set each of us into a particular personality type and make us noticeably similar to other individuals who share that particular type. Although the specific characteristics of each type I discuss here certainly won't sum up the whole of your personality or even of your specific type, they will reflect your general essence to a significant degree.

Within each basic type, of course, there's also a great deal of variation, and all of us may have a few characteristics of several types. Like people with AB blood, some of us are blends of two types, with one type a bit more predominating. My purpose here is not to delineate all the possible subtypes and variations—they are as infinite as people are unique—but rather to give you a general understanding of the nine major types of lovers: The Attention Seeker, The Emoter, The Cool Cucumber, The Perfectionist, The Skeptic, The Workaholic, The Controller, and The People Pleaser.

Looking at Your Partner or Potential Mate

When you're first falling in love, your partner can do no wrong. He's the smartest, the sweetest; she's the kindest, the most beautiful. Over time, however, you begin to focus on all the things that irritate and annoy you. Either way, you often miss seeing the whole picture. That's because each of us, no matter what our personality type, has both captivating characteristics and attributes that drive others (and ourselves) a little crazy. There's an upside and a downside to every personality type, and it is this mixture of fabulous and frustrating that initially captivates us, then keeps us engaged and growing in our love affairs and intimate relationships.

As you go through the description of each type, you'll probably discover that it's the very things that initially attract you that are also the very things which, over time, will come to irritate you and cause friction in your relationship. Don't be alarmed. No type is perfect, and it is these captivating yet irritating differences that are the grist for every relationship mill. They provide opportunities for deeper love, personal growth, and greater understanding.

Take Controllers, for example. They're great at keeping tabs on the time, organizing a drawer, filing paper, or leaving the window half-open at night so the ventilation is perfect. The upside to this is that they're wonderful to have around when, for example, you're being audited by the IRS and they have every receipt in perfect order, or you're stranded on a deserted stretch of freeway and they just happen to have the right wrench in that tool box in the trunk of their car. The downside is that they expect everyone else to abide by their standards and will be offended if you're three minutes late, even if it's because you were in an accident that almost severed your jugular vein, or if, God forbid, you filed the gas receipt in the wrong drawer.

Like Controllers, each type has its own issues and extreme reactions, and they continually bump up against our own issues and extreme reactions. If the issues that keep coming up only serve to build a mountain of frustration, you two won't be happy for long. But if, on the other hand, you can begin to see these differences as revealing of your different personality types, you can embark on an exciting process of getting to know another person at a deep and truly intimate level. Learning the difference between your own and your partner's personality type can be fascinating; after all, one of the joys of being in a relationship is that you get to know someone who isn't a clone of yourself.

Understanding the nine types of lovers can also influence your choice of a partner. My friend Bill, who's had a lot of trouble finding a steady relationship, told me that in order to help himself pick a truly compatible mate, he recently decided to reveal a family secret to each of the women he dated. With this in mind, after a couple of dates with each of his new romantic partners, he'd get around to mentioning that his father had been a manic-depressive, had spend most of his life on medication, and killed himself when Bill was fifteen. Since Bill's father's death was a gigantic emotional issue for Bill, he wanted to see how each of these women reacted.

One listened and then changed the subject to talk about the new computer she'd just bought. "It's got all the bells and whistles," she said, and she just couldn't wait to use it for the hundreds of sales graphs she'd be setting up at her new job.

Another said, "I'm so sorry, that must have been devastating."

Still another said, "Well, that was twenty years ago."

And the fourth one said, "You know, I just realized I've got an important call to make." She excused herself from the table and got up to use the phone in the restaurant.

By revealing a single, significant fact, Bill discovered what a wide range of responses people can have to almost any piece of information. Indeed, their responses were typical of four different personality types. The first woman was an Attention Seeker, the second a People Pleaser, the third a Cool Cucumber, and the fourth a Workaholic. As Bill listened to their responses, he realized that Woman #2 was far more attractive to him than all the others, even though initially his attraction had been strongest for Woman #1.

Just like Bill, the more we know about a given personality type, its usual distinguishing traits and what motivates people of this particular type, the better we can choose our partners and the more successful relationships we can have.

Learning how the captivating (and sometimes frustrating) characteristics of your partner's personality type engage with your own also opens a door to new possibilities in your relationships. Most of us want our partners to change in one way or another. If they don't we often get judgmental, nagging, demanding, or downright mean. We know somewhere in our hearts that these behaviors aren't helpful, but because we're frustrated, we don't know what else to do.

Paradoxically, it is through understanding and accepting how different your partner is from you that you can create the atmosphere for the greatest change. As you read this book, you will come to see that each personality type is struggling with a particular painful emotional issue. Understanding how the person you love got to be that way will instantly create some changes in your attitude. Instead of standing in judgment or trying to launch a campaign for behavior modification (you shouldn't do this, you better do that), you can start looking at the person you love with compassion. This in itself will create a new level of harmony in your relationship and increase the possibility that the changes you desire can actually occur. Nobody can change when there's a gun at their head. You couldn't. Neither can the person you love. Understanding, acceptance, forgiveness—these are the responses that create an atmosphere for change. And nothing can create that atmosphere more than understanding the basics of different personality types.

What About You?

Since a relationship is always a two-way street and a two-person affair, my purpose here isn't just to help you understand your romantic partner, or to encourage change in him or her, but also to encourage you to take a deeper look at yourself. What motivates you? What are your usual patterns of reacting and relating? What happened in your childhood? What is your life issue and how have you adapted to it? How have your personality characteristics affected the dynamics of your intimate relationships? These are some of the questions you'll have an opportunity to answer.

Looking at ourselves is sometimes difficult. We're so accustomed to seeing ourselves in a certain predictable way that we can't see certain things about ourselves that may be totally obvious to others. Or, we're so busy not liking what we see that we lose sight of how fine we really are. You can be so hung up on not having a college degree that you ignore how reliable you are, or you're so focused on your shyness that you ignore your ever-abundant empathy. Instead of seeing the unique and wonderful personality you do have, you tend to see only your faults. Or, on the other hand, instead of being willing to face a few glaring faults, you may tend to gloss them over, focusing instead on how smart or successful you are.

Whether you minimize or exaggerate your flaws, the obvious is often elusive. It's like that blind spot in your peripheral vision when you're driving a car. When I was taking driver's training, I was amazed to find out that no matter how often or carefully you look in the rear- and side-view mirrors, there's always a portion of the road or freeway you can't see, and that it's within this blind spot that an accident can most readily occur. In proof of the point, years later I had just such a "blind spot" accident.

It's the same with our personalities. While we may be aware of our conscious likes and dislikes—you like coffee, you don't eat sugar, you're a vegetarian, you like to vacation in the mountains, you like to vacation in Hawaii, you love dogs as opposed to cats, you have a pet snake, you'd never want to own your own home because of the burden of the mortgage, or, conversely, you wouldn't feel satisfied if you didn't own your own home—we may not be at all aware of the unconscious wounds that have shaped our personalities or molded them into their types.

Discovering Your Type

You'll notice as you check out the various types that it's probably much easier to identify the types of the people around you than to recognize your own. For example, your boss, Stan, is a Controller. He needs to know where every employee is at all times and has a terrible time giving up hands-on control of any project. Or your friend Bob is a Perfectionist. He's forty-two and has dated more women than Carter has liver pills, and none of them are good enough. Your ex-boyfriend, Phil, is an Attention Seeker. You praised him to the skies, gave him every gift his heart desired, and in spite of it all he never felt loved. Jane, your college roommate, was an inveterate Skeptic. Three (in your eyes, anyway) wonderful men asked her to marry them, but "It will never work out," she said sadly, each time she returned the engagement ring.

It's often easy to pick out these types. What is far more difficult, however, is discovering your own type. As you go through the list of personality types and the telltale traits for each, you'll be able to identify your type if you're a dead-ringer for three or four characteristics of that particular type. If only a single attribute seems to apply to you, most likely you're not this type but just have the normal amount of this particular trait in your overall personality. That's because all of us may have one or two of the characteristics of almost any type. And, as you will note, at the end of the description of each type there's an explanation of how the excessive characteristics of a particular type differ from the usual amount of those same attributes in most of the rest of us.

A second way you'll know is that as you read each list, certain traits that both the people who love you and even strangers have always appreciated or remarked about will suddenly jump out at you. That's another strong clue that this is your type. Or perhaps you'll just have a quiet feeling of recognition that says, "Oh, yes; this is me."

You may also note that you or your partner is a pretty obvious combination of two types; that is, that you move back and forth between two different types, or operate pretty much from two types simultaneously. This, like the AB blood type or the brown-haired blue-eyed person, is not the most familiar type, but if you strongly have two or three characteristics from two different types, it would be worthwhile for you to do the exercises that apply to both.

For example you may discover that you are an Emotive Attention Seeker—if you don't get the attention you need to feel loved, you start screaming or carrying on about it. Or you may be a Controlling People Pleaser. You want to make everybody else happy because your self-esteem isn't what you'd like it to be. But you've also learned to keep everything in your life under control to make up for your lack of feeling worthy, and you wish the people you love would learn to be as meticulous as you are.

Other common blends include Skeptical Cool Cucumbers, People-Pleasing Fantasizers, Attention-Seeking Controllers, and Workaholic or Controlling Perfectionists.

Whatever your type, if you want to have a better relationship, it's worth getting to know yourself as well as your partner. One caution, though: Let this be fun. The point of this book isn't to point a finger at your partner or beat yourself up, but to enjoyably discover more about yourself and, of course, to see how both you and your mate are operating in your relationship.

Once you've identified your type, you may want to ask yourself how your traits are affecting the relationship you are currently in—or, if you're not in a relationship at the moment, how your traits have specifically served to keep you out of one. Also, if you've recently—or even a long time ago—ended a relationship about which you still have emotional pain or which remains a mystery to you, it would be valuable to stop and identify your former partner's type, and then write about how your traits and theirs in combination contributed to that relationship's demise.

Coming Into Balance

In their classic form, all nine personality types represent some kind of extreme. As we become more aware of the difficult or harmful effects of these extremes, we can choose to move toward the middle of the personality curve and become a more balanced version of that particular type. The more we move toward the center, toward balance, the more we automatically become more giving and loving.

To this end, I've made a number of suggestions at the end of each chapter for modifying the negative aspects of each type. I've also suggested a brief meditation that will facilitate this movement toward change, and, finally, I've included a simple slogan or affirmation that you can repeat to yourself to secure the change in your consciousness.

The Challenge of Change

Change isn't always easy, but it is always possible. When I was in college, there was a very unpopular girl who irritated everybody by being an intellectual snob and a hopeless busybody. Every time she came into the commons for coffee, she would plunk herself down and bore everybody with her latest intellectual feat, while all the rest of us just wanted to have a cup of coffee, talk about Saturday's basketball game, and dream about where we were going on spring vacation. She irritated everyone, but eventually she "got it" that the minute she appeared in the commons, everybody took a dive under the table, trying to avoid her like the plague.

One day she asked me out to coffee, with the express purpose, she stated, of having me tell her why she turned everybody off when she was trying so hard to have friends. While I was a little taken aback by the directness of her request, I nevertheless admired her courage, and so I agreed to get together with her.

A few days later we had a very honest conversation in which I told her that people really did want to be her friends. In fact, they'd be happy to get to know her, but it would probably work better if she didn't tell us how she'd written the greatest philosophy paper on Earth, aced her latest math test, or made 99 percentile on her Graduate Record Exams. We weren't intrigued by all that; in fact, we were put off by the endless recitation of her achievements. The rest of us were struggling to do as well as we could in school and in our off time we just wanted to hang around and get to know one another. It would be nice, I suggested, if once in a while, she'd inquire about somebody else. "What did you think about the math test, Jack?" Or "I'm sorry to hear your father died, Lee."

I suppose this classic Attention Seeker was one of my first "clients." It was beautiful, as time went on, to see how she changed. Not long after our little heart-to-heart conversation, she started inviting people to coffee and even asking them questions about themselves. When one of her roommates ended up in the infirmary, she brought her a card and some flowers. She even changed her image, started reading *Mademoiselle* along with Chaucer, and actually went to a basketball game.

As I watched her transform, I developed great admiration for her. She had the courage to find out where she was going awry and, once having gotten the message, to change. Two years later, when she graduated as the valedictorian of her class, it wasn't her academic record but the friendships she had made that turned out to be the crowning achievement of her college career.

Like this young woman, many of us have a blind spot about ourselves that holds us back from creating the kind of relationships we long for. We don't like to admit it, and it's not because we're stubborn or mean-spirited, but just because it's so hard to see who we really are. It's always easier to see another person, especially when we're in a relationship. After all, we're faced with their dirty laundry every day, the newspaper they insist on leaving rumpled up next to the big chair in the living room, the mail they keep piling atop the kitchen counter mixed up with last night's dinner dishes.

Still, by looking at others, we can develop our powers of observation, and the more aware we become about them, the more we can discover about ourselves. By observing how they interact with others, how they express their feelings, how they work in a calm, steady manner, or blow up at the drop of a hat, we start getting the gist of how people behave. And once we've developed that capacity for observation, we can turn it around and take an honest look at ourselves. When we're finally able to do this, we suddenly see that our own personality traits, our habits and behaviors, our attitudes and life issues, have just as much impact on the person we're loving as their attributes have on us. Not only that, but we see that any relationship is the dynamic interplay of another person's attributes with us, and ours with them.

The beautiful thing about this process is that the more we become aware of how our own personalities contribute to the dynamics of a relationship, the more we can change and, like my college friend, the more we can learn how to love. Instead of complaining and insisting that the other person change, the more we modify our own behavior, the more actual change can occur in our relationships.

Self-awareness, being able to see who we are and what we're doing, is perhaps the greatest influence in each of our relationships. Indeed, it is often this lack of self-knowledge which prevents love from coming toward us, or, once it has arrived, keeps it from reaching its fullest potential. And so, any effort you make toward self-awareness will be a powerful gift to your relationship.

As you will see, each personality type has uniquely positive attributes and also specific limitations. These limitations, the things about each of us that drive our partners crazy, represent not only familiar points of frustration in a relationship, but also your personal growing edge. They define the arena in which, in any particular relationship, you are being challenged to grow.

Relationships as Evolution

Finally, we need to remember that we're all going through a process of evolution in our relationships. Each time your personality type engages with another, you can't help but grow. It may not always be fun; it may be a gigantic challenge, but precisely because of the relationships we are in, we become more and more developed as human beings, and ultimately, become able to give the unique gifts that are ours to give in this lifetime.

This process is why we are alive. It's why we have personalities in the first place. We discover the world through them; we fall in love because of them; we move toward our higher spiritual selves through them; and in the end we'll discover that they're all a part of God, no matter how magnificent or peculiar they might be.

My fond hope is that understanding these nine personality types will enable you to love more deeply, with a greater measure of ease, and with the gracefulness that comes from knowing your own and your partner's roles in the dynamics of your relationship. By understanding yourself and your partner better, you can make your relationship a place where both of your personalities can blossom, and where that mysterious and beautiful gift—Love—can rise to its highest level of expression.

1

THE ATTENTION SEEKER

"Enough about me; let's talk about you.
What do *you* think of *me?*"

ATTENTION SEEKERS ARE THE FASCINATING, VIVID
personalities of the relationship wheel. Often incredibly creative, they always have an idea or a project. Exciting and
energetic, they intrigue and amuse the rest of us with their
endless, intricate renditions of the ups and downs of their
lives. Their environments are alive with creativity and action.

These are the great achievers of the personality types.
Because they're extremely good at focusing on what is important to them, they can be inspired by an idea and marshal all
their forces to pursue it. We are fascinated by them, because
single-handedly they seem to create a world of their own and
their worlds are always complex and unendingly fascinating.
We feel lucky, privileged even, when they invite us to share in

their lives. Compared to our own, the universes they create seem brilliant, mysterious, and exciting. Artists, writers, musicians, and charismatic leaders are often Attention Seekers. Because of their remarkable self-focus, they can direct their energy with laser-point intensity on whatever they seek to do.

They are also incredibly good at attracting others. Their ability to focus on their own concerns and believe that whatever they're doing is important is in itself enough to engage the support of everyone around them. This, combined with their talent, often leads to stunning achievement. They never tire of their own new ideas and undertakings or of corralling you into their projects. In time, though, their never-ending self-focus can become tedious and even painful to those they have gathered around them.

Claire, a fabric designer, created her first remarkable designs on paper bags when she was still a teenager. Everyone at school was intrigued, and Claire lost no time in collecting money from all her friends so she could go to New York and try her hand in the big fish pond of fashion design. There were pitfalls along the way, of course. Some of her designs were stolen—well, actually, she lost them in a phone booth. But everyone back home had to hear about her little career catastrophe ad nauseam, curse the thief, and then laugh at her mistake when a kindly stranger returned them.

During this time, Claire's best friend's father died back home, but Claire couldn't go to the funeral—she couldn't afford even an economy ticket, and besides she was too busy chasing down her lost designs. One way or another she was so embroiled in her own undertakings that she also forgot to send a card.

Because of her drive, Claire finally "made it." In a couple of years, she was a roaring success and when she had her first major sale, she invited everyone to New York for a party. Thinking she would thank them for their support, her friends all bought plane tickets and came, but when they arrived, all she could do was regale them with the blow-by-blow account of her rise to success. Still, they were happy to have been invited—her world was far more interesting than theirs. And when she was written up in *Vogue* a few months later, they all dropped her name and said how great it was to know her.

Telltale Signs of an Attention Seeker

- You are brilliant, highly focused, and very creative.
- Others are drawn to your energy and undertakings.
- You are concerned with how others see you.
- You have a number of people who gather around you, but when you really think about it, how well do you know any of them?
- You have difficulty listening, empathizing, or supporting others when they have problems.
- You have trouble handling criticism.
- Deep down you feel that, just as yourself, you were never loved.
- You feel like you can never get enough praise or support.

A Closer Look: Distinguishing Characteristics of Attention Seekers

1 The attention seeker is very good at seeing him- or herself and not nearly as good at seeing others.

In psychological terms, the issue Attention Seekers struggle with is narcissism. This word comes from Greek mythology and refers to a handsome young man, Narcissus, who, in searching for himself, became so captivated by his own reflection in a pool that he finally fell in and drowned.

Like Narcissus, the Attention Seeker is predominantly involved with self: *my* problems, the phone call *I* didn't get, *my* job, *my* raise, *my* pain, the dress *I'm* going to wear to the party. While of course all of us are very interested in ourselves and our problems, Attention Seekers are overly involved with themselves, unable to focus attention away from themselves and onto others for any significant length of time.

Even when the Attention Seeker endeavors to engage with another, it's usually for the purpose of gaining further awareness or benefit to himself. The Attention Seeker isn't aware that she doesn't really want to get to know another person, but somehow or other, her behavior always leads back to self. Just as all roads lead to Rome, all conversations for the Attention Seeker lead back to himself. It's somehow just too much trouble for the Attention Seeker to get to know another person. Maybe there isn't time—sometimes that's their excuse—but even if there's time, there certainly isn't the inclination.

2 Attention Seekers have trouble with empathy, that special quality of human interaction of "feeling for" another person.

If you say to one of them, "I'm devastated because I had a frightening car accident. I've got a whiplash injury and I'm afraid my neck will be knotted up for life," instead of empathetically saying, "I'm so sorry. That sounds frightening. Is there anything I can do?" the Attention Seeker will bring the attention back to herself. "That reminds me of *my* car accident," she'll say. "I had really bad whiplash, and I'm still not over it." Or, "Oh, that's nothing compared to the time I stubbed my toe." The other response of the Attention Seeker is, "It's no big deal." Or, "You'll get over it." Whatever their response, the Attention Seeker moves as quickly as possible from the uncomfortable position of having to offer empathy and back to the comfortable position of talking about him- or herself.

A corollary of this is that Attention Seekers aren't good listeners. While they expect *you* to listen with blaring enthusiasm and of course a wealth of praise, empathy, and suggestions as to how they might solve their myriad problems —they can't get enough of your admiration of their new bathing suit, the paint job on their wall, the job they just got, their purple nail polish, the way they conducted their last seminar or told off their mother-in-law—the Attention Seeker has a very short fuse when it comes to listening to you. Like a firecracker already lit by a match, there's barely a moment's silence, now that the wick is burning, before the narcissistic Attention Seeker is ready to pop off again with his own slew of needs, concerns, and requirements for reassurance.

3 Attention Seekers project that they are deserving and self-confident.

Since they always seem to be so involved with what they're doing, getting, or being at the moment, they project an image of feeling worthy and self-confident. Because they appear to value themselves, we're inclined to value them too. They broadcast the message that somehow their position should be supported, that their self-involvement is definitely justified, and that we should give them all the attention they want and need.

4 Attention Seekers are also good at complaining about others, particularly about how others have failed them.

Because Attention Seekers project deservingness and self-confidence, they appear justified in their complaints about any- and everyone who has failed to give them the attention, support, and nurturance they so obviously need and deserve.

This feeling about the legitimacy of complaining springs, as we shall see, from a deep-seated feeling of not being loved. While not in touch with this feeling, Attention Seekers treat everybody around them, including virtual strangers, as if they owed the Attention Seeker the undivided and unconditional love that can only reasonably be expected from parents.

5 Attention Seekers are emotionally fragile.

Though they don't appear to be to the rest of us, due to their strong capacity to enlist support, Attention Seekers are very emotionally fragile and brittle inside. Inside they're not really sure that everything they do is all the great shakes they say it is. That is precisely why they are constantly asking for praise, support, and reassurance.

6 Attention Seekers identify with their achievements rather than with their spirits.

Attention Seekers are always trying to get attention because deep down they aren't sure they have value just as the people they are. By over-identifying with what they do, they are able to gain some limited sense of their own worth to make up for their wound of feeling unloved.

Why We Love Attention Seekers

We like to be around Attention Seekers because they're always cooking up something new. They capture our attention because of the exciting things they're doing. We love to listen to the at first really engaging stories they endlessly tell about themselves. They're important to themselves and important in the world, and we like to be around such obviously interesting and important people. Like the captain of the football team that every high school girl is dying to go out with, we want to be connected to Attention Seekers, because they're doing something of note and we want to bask in their glory.

They're also very good at creating colorful pictures of their worlds and inviting the rest of us in to have a look at their exciting lives. We love to taste of their worlds, either vicariously or firsthand, because they're so alive, unusual, and fascinating.

We also like to love them because they project an apparently unflappable sense of their own value. Most of us don't feel that self-confident, nor do we feel secure in outright asking for as much support and approval as Attention Seekers so easily do. Being in the aura of an Attention Seeker therefore inspires the rest of us to ask for more, to see the legitimacy of marshaling support on our own behalf, and to be more direct in asking for it.

How They Drive Us Crazy

Attention Seekers are energy sappers. In their endless need for affirmation and attention they drain us; we tire of how involved with themselves they continue to be. There's only room for one person in a relationship with a Attention Seeker—and that's the Attention Seeker.

Because of their tendency to make servants of the people around them, Attention Seekers tend to exhaust the people who love them and ultimately to lose the genuine attention and affection of the people they draw into their friendships and intimate relationships. Finally, the person who loves the Attention Seeker becomes exhausted, and, following the Attention Seeker's example cries, "What about ME!" Thus the person related to the Attention Seeker receives the gift that only the Attention Seeker can give: instruction in how to develop a measure of self-concern and self-focus, which might well have been lacking before the Attention Seeker arrived on the scene to demonstrate what it looks like.

Attention Seekers sabotage relationships with their self-focus because they lack some of the deeper skills required to have a balanced relationship, specifically, the ability to give *and* take, to speak *and* listen, to nurture *as well as* be nurtured, to empathize with *as well as* swim in the constant river of empathy flowing toward them.

What's Really Going On?

To all outside observers, Attention Seekers seem just fine. They're so busy being concerned about themselves and so apparently puffed up with their own egos that it's hard to believe they could have a problem in the world. Anybody who is always asking, "What should I do about . . ." or, "What do you think of my. . ." or saying, "We've got to go back to the house; I forgot my vitamins!" not only seems to be, but is, in fact, so obviously able to take care of themselves on so many levels that it's hard to believe that anything else could be going on with them. Their unending requests for feedback, reassurance, admiration, praise, notice, and attention make observers of Attention Seekers feel that they are really doing just fine. But these multitudinous requests for attention and shoring up actually belie a deeper level of insecurity.

If we look a little deeper we see that, inside, the Attention Seeker is really very fragile and feels unequipped to cope with life. Despite all their efforts at self-attention, Attention Seekers feel as if they have never gotten enough attention to be able to handle another person's reality. Although they seem self-confident and strong, perfectly at ease with using up all the airtime, inside they feel inadequate, unable to create a strong enough sense of self, or "ego structure," as the psychologists would call it, to hold their own ground in the presence of another person's ego.

They don't want to get too deeply involved with another person because they feel emotionally unprepared for it. They wouldn't know what to do if they actually encountered another person's concerns about *her* dress, *her* flabby thighs, *her* cavorting husband, the job *he* lost or *his* mother's alcoholism. Unconsciously they fear that they can't be effective in dealing with anyone else, because deep down they feel as if they still haven't received enough themselves to be of use or service to another.

The Attention Seeker's emotional wound is a profound lack of love. As human beings, we deserve to be loved simply because we're alive and we are who we are. This pure, unconditional positive acceptance is what love in fact is, and it is everyone's birthright. We deserve to be loved not because we've won the gold medal, made it onto the winning hockey team, or won the beauty contest, but simply because we're here as ourselves, and unconditional love is the appropriate response to our existence.

When we experience unconditional love—the simple, heartfelt love of parents—everything in our lives makes sense. We know we're okay. We know that our achievements are not as important as our emotions and our spirits, and that whatever we do, whatever the size of the mark that we make, we, just as ourselves, have value.

When this love is not present, the Attention Seeker thinks that he or she has to do something to attain it or to be worthy of it. Here begins the endless effort to accomplish (and the attendant cry for affirmation that is so typical of the narcissistic Attention Seeker). Basically, all the Attention Seeker needs to know is, *It's okay that I'm here,* and *Just as myself, I am loved.* But because Attention Seekers' parents in some way suffered from a lack of love, they often pass on this wound. They themselves may have had parents who confused the value of achievement with the beauty of just pure being. As a result, instead of knowing the precious worthiness of living their own essence, Attention Seekers live in the hellish confusion of endlessly wondering if their worth resides in who they are or what they have done. They need, very simply, for no reason (and every reason) to be loved. To be received back into the nourishing nest of unconditional love.

I know a lovely young Narcissist who is forever complaining about her father, whom she says is so self-righteous, self-involved, and achievement-oriented that he's blind to her every need. "I don't know why he can't see what I need," she wails over and over again—after he's given her a credit card, a new car for college, and total support while she went to look at the thirteen different colleges she was considering.

"All he ever thinks about is himself," she says. "He's so busy with his law practice, his new wife, and their new baby that he never thinks of me," she says, calling her friends at all hours of the day and night, waking their babies, interrupting their quiet evenings at home to talk about the colleges she just visited, the wardrobes she would wear to each, and how she'll spend her monthly allowance.

Her parents were divorced when she was an infant and, as a consequence of their involvement with their own issues, she never felt secure in their love. Consequently she is the mirror-image of her father's own overinvolvement and is desperately seeking his attention, the same attention he never got from his father, a busy politician who was always so concerned about doing his job well and gaining the vote of his constituents that he never had time to be with his children.

As this young woman's story demonstrates, Attention Seekers are often the children of Attention Seekers. What this means is that one or both of their parents were so overly self-involved that, rather than having time to love or nurture their child, they were worried about themselves. During all the stages of development when the child needed the inner feeling of being loved just for himself, his parents were off on a narcissistic venture of their own. Instead of being able to nurture their child's development, this development remained unsupported. As a result, the Attention Seeker feels insecure inside, even though objectively he or she is most likely a very talented and capable person.

For example, Jake's mother, a fashion model who gave birth to Jake at age thirty-eight, resented him from the outset for the distortion of her figure caused by her pregnancy. For years she had been the focus of international attention, and her sense of identity rested heavily on her perception of herself as a shapely and beautiful woman.

From the moment Jake was born, she tried in every way possible to regain her lost youth and her sense of herself as beautiful. While she was in fact still beautiful, the impact of her pregnancy so distorted her perception of herself that she kept constantly looking for reassurance from Jake's father and later on, from him.

Little Jake didn't have a mother; rather he became his mother's mirror. All the things he needed to be told about himself—that he was a sweet-natured, smart boy, that he was doing well in school, that his mother was proud of him and was glad he was born—she unconsciously but consistently withheld. Because he was bright, he succeeded in spite of this painful lack of attention. He went on to do very well in school and indeed, because of his intellectual brilliance, became the valedictorian of his high school and then of his college. All the while, though, he continually asked his schoolmates, friends, and sweethearts to stroke his ego by telling him how brilliant he was, and to join him in putting down anyone else who came close to being as talented as he was.

While Jake has attracted many lovers and friends because of his creativity and brilliance—he's now a successful journalist—his intimate relationships have always been disasters. Sooner or later they all dwindle into a chorus of requests for bolstering his male ego, telling him how great he is. "Did you see my article on the Sand Fly in the *Sunday Post*?" "Did you know I've got an in with the *Chronicle*?" "The editor at *LIFE* just loved my piece on stock market stress; they'll want me on the staff any day now, don't you think?"

While Jake is successful in work, he hasn't been very successful in love. He doesn't understand why a man with all his credentials and achievements couldn't attract a great woman, so he continues asking all his friends to tell him not what's the matter with him, but how great he is, and to assure him that at any minute the girl of his dreams will step across the threshold of his life.

Then there's Fred. Both of Fred's parents were vaudeville performers. His mother was a sexy dish and his father a fancy dancer. They did the circuit and got rave reviews; the birth of little Freddy put a crimp in their style. Rather than settling down or developing a different pair of careers, Freddy's parents dragged him along to all their shows. He never felt that he was important just as himself. In twelve years he went to sixteen schools. As he grew up, his mother, whose beauty was fading from the long roads and the long hard life, used to ask Freddy to sit in the dressing room with her and tell her a million times a day how pretty she still was. His father, meanwhile, taught him dancing, but always told him that he wasn't now and never would be as good a dancer as he was.

When Freddy grew up, he wanted to become an actor. He had showtime in his blood. By then his parents had died, but Freddy still felt unloved. Unlike Jake, who couldn't keep a girl for long, Freddy married young. An electrician by trade, he studied acting, continually putting his family in financial jeopardy with his expensive acting lessons and repeated forays to photographers for head shots and casting calls a hundred miles away. While Freddy's family suffered, just as he had as a child, he would read his parts at the dinner table, asking his wife and children to applaud, until exhausted by Freddy's seemingly endless need to perform and be praised, his wife "abruptly" left him after nine years of marriage.

Sometimes the Attention Seeker's wound isn't the direct result of a narcissistic parent but rather of a family situation which, in itself, precludes the giving of appropriate support. In a situation where there isn't enough love to go around, a child can also suffer the deep emotional wound of feeling unloved.

Take Carrie, for example. Her older brother was a schizophrenic who created so much havoc in the family that during all the years of her growing up, he alone was the focus of attention. It was always, "What's Bobby going to do next?" "How is he going to act? Is he going to come home and shoot Mom and Dad the way he threatens to every other week?" Even though his behavior was negative, he took up so much attention in the family circle that Carrie never received the nurturing and support she needed to get a sense that she counted, that she had value—in short, that she was loved.

Her brother's illness, which emerged when she was four, and became significant when she was ten, continued to sap the family's energies through all her years at home. Unable to get the love she needed, Carrie became desperate inside. She was also continually worried about whether or not she could actually stand on her own two feet when she became an adult or would have something worthwhile to contribute. Thus she started down the narcissistic trail of asking everyone who crossed her path for the support, reassurance, and indulgence that she unconsciously hoped would make her feel strong and loved enough to gain a footing in her own life.

No matter the precise circumstances that create the Attention Seeker's void of love, these often gifted people are struggling to know that they are all right just as they are.

Nothing can make up for love, and the Attention Seeker's tragedy is that they, too, often mistake worlds of attention for the pure, heartfelt, and unconditional love they so desperately need.

The Difference Between an Attention Seeker and Everyone Else

The Attention Seeker is willing to live in self-focus, while the rest of us only need to visit there. While it is appropriate from time to time for all of us to be totally focused on ourselves, the rest of us know that love is a give and take, and that in the rhythm of our relationships we move back and forth from focus on ourselves to focus on others.

In fact, it is this ability to at times be the object of another's focus and to sometimes willingly give the gift of focus to another that constitutes the emotional exchange of a relationship. It's the way both people in a relationship can thrive and survive.

What Attention Seekers Have to Teach Us

What we can all learn from the Attention Seeker is how to take better care of ourselves. We can also learn that a certain amount of self-focus is appropriate. Attention Seekers teach us that what we're good at is worth pursuing, that focus leads to results. Their genius inspires us. In addition, in their seemingly endless and intricate focus upon themselves, Attention Seekers delight us by exposing us to many nooks and crannies of personality and of life itself, worlds and concerns that non-Attention Seekers never bother to give attention to.

We learn about the complexity of life from them: how our dresses, houses, children, friends, lovers, strangers, environments, vacations, vitamin regimens, exercise routines, hair styles, nail polish can affect us, make our lives more interesting and textured, and be topics of interest in our lives and conversations.

With their inordinate focus on everything that touches their lives, Attention Seekers show us how rich and varied our own lives can be.

What Attention Seekers Need to Learn About Relationships

Attention Seekers need to remember that relationships are a two-way street. Intimacy, that feeling of love and closeness we all cherish, is developed not only when we get what we need, but also when we discover ourselves as being able to give what others need. Love and pleasure in a relationship occur when we can experience ourselves as loving people. The more love that's being offered—the more attention, affection, affirmation, encouragement, support, empathy, listening, response that's being shared both ways—the more closely connected and harmonious people feel.

Attention seekers need to give the love that they themselves need. Then they will receive it.

What Attention Seekers Can Do to Come Into Balance

1 Listen.

Attention Seekers will start joining in the pleasures of relationships when they learn to listen, not just to the answers that are focused on themselves, but also to the information that reveals who other people are. We miss a chance at getting acquainted with how fascinating other people are if we're only interested in *their* responses to *us*. People can tell you the most surprising things about themselves, what they're doing, and where they're headed if only you can let go of the fear that you'll become invisible by listening. Instead of worrying about yourself, take the opportunity to be entertained by others.

Recently, on the beach, I saw a little girl whose mother was obviously an Attention Seeker. "How's my tan?" she kept asking. "Am I getting a sunburn? Should I put more lotion on? When's Daddy coming back from lunch?" She never stopped to listen long enough to hear her daughter say, "Mommy, I just saw a great big turtle in the water! It was beautiful and had a big green shell and flippers!"

2 Ask questions.

Because of endlessly looking at themselves and having everybody else look at them, the Attention Seeker's world grows smaller and smaller. So, if you want to be delivered from the burden and the loneliness of your narcissism (because narcissism does leave people very lonely), start asking questions in all your encounters: How are you? What's going on in your life? What has interested you lately? What's your favorite food?

Taking the risk of becoming acquainted with other people will allow you to see that your own ego is strong enough to continue standing when you take the risk of truly knowing others. The more you venture into inquiring about other people, the more you'll have an opportunity to see how interesting they are and how interesting life is. This is part of the richness of love.

3 Respond.

As we've already said, Attention Seekers are afraid of knowing about other people because their deep inner fear is that they don't have the emotional resources with which to respond. Remember that *any genuine response creates closeness.* It doesn't have to be perfect, it just needs to be real. It can even be a fragmented or stuttering attempt to offer empathy or support. It's the kindness of the effort that counts.

When your best friend's mother dies, instead of saying nothing, because inside you feel inadequate, try saying "I heard your mother died, and I really don't know what to say. I've never been through that. I guess all I can say is, I'm sorry." Or, when a person tells you about their illness or exhaustion, instead of saying, "That reminds me of my illness," say, "I'm sorry. Do you feel like talking about it? I'd like to listen."

4 Learn empathetic phrases.

"I'm so sorry. That sounds terrible." "I'm so happy for you. I'm delighted you're having a wonderful vacation." "Your new job sounds fabulous. Congratulations!" Whenever we offer these phrases we show people that we're somehow inside of their reality with them. The beautiful thing about this is, it's not just that we're being masters of empathy and *they* don't feel alone anymore, but *we* don't feel alone anymore either. Whenever you throw a rope to somebody else to save them, you're also saving them to be your companion in life. If they're gone forever, so is your pleasure in them.

The Attention Seeker always feels like the person who wants to send a sympathy card to the family of the man who was killed in a car crash, but is so afraid she won't say the right thing that she never sends the card at all. The truth is, a heartfelt "I'm so sorry" can bring you into closeness until such time as you can develop the skills of saying something more intricate.

5 Praise others.

Start now and do this exercise every day. At least once a day, take note of one attribute in another person that is worthy and notable, and praise it. You'll see that your own attributes of excellence don't disappear and that, far from finding yourself on the ever-shaky footing of an Attention Seeker, the more generous you can be in praising others, the more quietly and strongly you can stand in solid awareness of yourself.

Once again, praising, acknowledging, giving the response that you yourself are always asking for, will create a sense of well-being in you. Instead of feeling like a desperate, fragile Attention Seeker who needs to be endlessly shored up, you will realize through the strength of your giving that other people are drawn toward you and that they will *naturally* give you the responses you need.

6 Learn to take criticism.

Since internally, Attention Seekers feel they're standing on shaky ground with their own egos, it's extremely difficult for them to hear criticism. It's as if they're constantly saying, "If you can't praise me, if you're not on my side, if you don't think I'm great, then get off my tennis court because I'm too fragile to improve."

Constructive criticism is just that: constructive. It tells us how our own position can get stronger, if we're just willing to listen and make some adjustments. So, take a deep breath, let the criticism enter, and make an honest attempt to implement its content. If the person says to you, "You're always talking about yourself and frankly I'm sick of listening," make a conscious attempt next time, once you've asked for advice or support, to return the favor by asking, "Is there anything I can do for you?" Or, take a deep breath, look at your watch and decide that for five minutes you're going to listen to anything they have to say and when they're finished, give them the appropriate response. Whether that's "Wow, that's great news," or, "I'm sorry to hear how tough the last two weeks have been for you," let them hear back from you.

Attention Seekers need to slow down and be aware that the world isn't going to collapse if 15,000 people aren't telling them every five minutes that they're okay. If you leave some little spaces in the conversation, and stop lobbying for all the responses you think you can't live without, you'll discover that other people can step into these little spaces and teach you something new. Instead of all your dialogues being about you, you might hear about someone else's extraordinary spiritual experience, the way they met a personal challenge (and have thereby set an example for you), or how all of us ought to get serious about preparing for Y2K.

7 Be straightforward about your need for love.

Since the Attention Seeker's great wound is that he or she wasn't loved well enough, a lot of begging for attention can be avoided if the Attention Seeker can learn to say simply: "Please tell me that you love me." Or, even more simply, "I need your love."

A Meditation for Attention Seekers

I will feel loved when I remember that I need to give as well as get attention. My relationship will grow through my generosity to others. The more I can take the attention off myself and give my attention to others, the better the relationship I'll have. When I am loving, I will feel loved.

Balancing Affirmations

The person I love isn't just like me.

Other people have needs too.

When I give love, I will feel loved.

2

THE EMOTER

"Take it to the limit one more time."

EMOTERS ARE THE FIERY SUPERNOVAS OF THE personality spectrum. Dramatic and flamboyant, they light up every room with their energetic presence. Emotion is the life they live, the air they breathe; and the louder, the longer, the stronger, the better. The word *emotion* comes from the Latin meaning "to move out from" and the Emoter is constantly moving energy and feelings out of his body and into the surrounding environment.

Emoters are fun to be around, for with an Emoter, everything is an adventure of epic proportions. The Emoter is a drama queen, prone to exaggeration—she has always had the *worst* day, the *best* train ride, the *most* fabulous chocolate soufflé. He lost a *million* dollars (it was actually $1,000); she had 500 phone calls to return (well, fifteen). They make

41

great sales people, PR people, agents, managers, and cheer-leaders; they do well in any profession that requires hype and hoopla, the building up of something or someone. They are often very inspirational, for they are masters at using emotion to create effect.

Emoters can be very charming, drawing you into their whirlwind of energy. You may not like the level of energy they put out, but it will captivate you anyway, because its sheer intensity will lift you to heights where, just on your own, you'd never dare to go.

There's nothing hidden about an Emoter, nothing subterranean or below the surface. You know you're with an Emoter when you meet someone who always lets you hear how they feel in no uncertain terms. They don't hold back. When you leave an encounter with an Emoter, you never have to worry that there is something they're not telling you. If they feel it, believe me, you'll hear about it. Unlike Attention Seekers, Emoters just need to express their feelings—strongly. Once they do, they can actually come around and listen to you because they've had their emotional thrills.

Katherine is a charming, witty Emoter who, fresh out of college, started at the bottom of the ladder at a large book publishing firm. Now thirty-five, she's just been named publicity director. She got where she is so fast because she's a fast-talking, emotionally vibrant publicist. Jaded TV and radio producers, caught up in her whirlwind of enthusiasm, book her authors more often than anyone else's. The same is true with prospective lovers—she exudes so much charm and energy that they can't help but be captivated. But if you cross her, watch out—she'll come right at you, finger pointed, and tell you dramatically and loudly just what you've done wrong. She often uses empty threats—"I'll quit," "I'll leave you"—in the heat of the moment. When confronted later, she says she didn't really mean it.

Telltale Signs of an Emoter

- You both feel and express emotions intensely.

- You cry and/or scream a lot.

- You create relationship dramas.

- You like the experience of heightened feelings.

- You believe that other people aren't emotional enough.

- You express the feelings for everybody in the relationship.

A Closer Look: Distinguishing Characteristics of Emoters

1 The Emoter is overly emotional.

In psychological terms, Emoters are hysterics. They always seem to want to go into deep emotional waters or respond to every situation with "their feelings." They won't just tell you, either; they will *show* you just how good or how bad they feel. They have the feelings that most of the rest of us would just as soon avoid or keep only for special occasions. The expression, "You don't have to make a federal case out of everything!" applies pretty regularly to an Emoter. Emoters seem to "go off" at the drop of a hat, creating dramas about every single thing that occurs to them or in a relationship.

2 Everything affects them emotionally, and they need you to hear about it.

Emoters always want you to know how they feel. And it isn't enough just to state their case or to quietly register an opinion, they have to create a scene, scream, yell, threaten, or throw pans, let you know that what you did was totally unforgivable, off the charts, and you may have to crawl over broken glass to get into their good graces again. At the further reaches, they may resort to physical abuse.

To them, everything is an opportunity for an emotional free-for-all. Nothing gets by their emotional Richter scale. An emotional earthquake that could topple a major city barely comes to the bottom line of their measuring instruments. They're always having a reaction to something and ninety times out of a hundred, it's intense. "What do you mean, it doesn't matter?" or, "How could you possibly do that to me?" These are the familiar battle cries of a good garden-variety Emoter.

To the Emoter, everything is a catastrophe. It isn't just, "My husband's forty minutes late coming home from work," it's, "He's crashed on the freeway and burned, I'm never going to see him again!" It isn't, "She spent too much money on the credit cards," it's, "We're going to the poorhouse. She's driving us bankrupt." And in expressing their feelings about the catastrophe, they often say things they later claim they didn't really mean—that they're going to leave you, that you're the worst person in the world, that they're going to jump off the bridge because of what you did. While they want you to take their feelings very seriously when they're upset, they're often flabbergasted when later you're still hurting from something they said hours ago in the heat of the moment.

While Emoters tend to love the world of emotion and especially their own emotional expression, each one tends to have a particular emotion in which he becomes a specialist.

For example, some Emoters are whiners. I know one with whom you can never have a conversation but that her life is always just about to fall off the edge of the cliff: fourteen unbelievable things have happened, her blood sugar is out of control, her boyfriend has just left her, the icebox blew up, the gardener hasn't showed up for weeks and the grass is growing up to the windowsills. Besides that, her daughter has disowned her, she's fatter than she's ever been, and, by the way, why haven't you called her lately to find out all of the above?

Another sub-type of Emoter is the yellers and slammers. These Emoters only know they've felt something if they've raised their voices, yelled their heads off, and made the windows clatter in their frames or the neighbors tremble under their down comforters. The same goes with slamming doors, backing the truck out of the driveway spitting gravel like dragon tongues, or throwing the frying pan across the room. These behaviors have the effect of heightening the excitement for the Emoter and, of course, of terrifying anybody in their proximity.

Other Emoters are verbal abusers. They get their emotional rocks off by saying something really mean and nasty that cuts to the psychic quick of another person. It's as if they know exactly where everybody's emotional Achilles heel is. They dive for the jugular and never miss. They are psychic sure shots, usually without being consciously aware of it; the devastating truth wells up in them like the lava in Vesuvius, and they just let it rip. This sub-type's outbursts have a cutting edge that never fails to assassinate a person's character or pierce someone through at the point of their greatest vulnerability.

Still other Emoters are sobbers and criers. Anything you say hurts their feelings, and they have to cry about it right now and in your presence. Maybe it'll be a little trickle of tears that can make you feel sorry for them, but most of the time it will be good roaring sobs that will make you feel as if you have to take care of them—you've done an unforgivable thing, and God help you now, because it's up to you to find a way to make them stop crying.

Finally, other Emoters are throwers. They don't feel they've expressed their feelings unless they've broken something, ripped it to shreds, tied you up with it, or watched it land on the far side of the room. Now you "get" how bad they feel about whatever it is that happened, what you just did to them, or what isn't happening in your relationship. Like the spear hurlers of old, they get their point across by launching some object into orbit, thereby letting you know that you have crossed some invisible line.

3 Emoters believe that feelings are all that matters.

In fact, you can often identify an Emoter or overly emotional person because they're always using phrases like, "Well, these are just my feelings." Or, "Don't *you* have any feelings about what's just happened?" "You don't even know what it is to feel." Emoters don't know it, but these fiery moments are what they live for. Since they are feeling types, when emotions are present and in abundance, Emoters are happy.

Raw emotion is the medium of exchange for the Emoter. They love to express their passion, fear, anger, and even excitement very intensely, and they are suspect and judgmental of people who don't feel as intensely as they do.

4 Emoters love to create dramas.

Since the meat and potatoes of any Emoter's emotional life is an intense emotional experience, they don't know what to do with themselves if it's a calm and beautiful day. As a result, if a drama isn't happening, they often go to unconscious extremes to create one—so they can feel that life is interesting and that something is, in fact, going on. I call this created or instigated drama "the passionate encounter."

What I mean by this is that by bringing up some emotional issue—"What do you mean it's not a big deal that we're two dollars in debt?"—the Emoter will cook up a fray that will, eventually, engage the naturally offended, exasperated, or intense response of their partner. When this exchange hits high pitched levels, the Emoter has created a level of emotional exchange that feels familiar. It is precisely through this level of intensity that Emoters feel emotionally connected to their partners.

5 Emoters thrive on loss of control.

Because feelings are so all-important to the Emoter and because feelings are the antithesis of reason, Emoters thrive on loss of control. The calm complacency or quiet unfolding of the process of a relationship seems boring, uninteresting, or maybe even unreal to them. In fact, when everything's out of control, this feels natural and normal. They often don't know what another person's talking about if they're just talking. And when they themselves are shrieking their heads off, they often think they're "just having a conversation." Afterward, as if they've had a lapse of memory, they will report the experience as if they were simply "telling the other person how they felt." This loss of control by letting it go with feelings is so familiar to Emoters that they can't recognize it as an out-of-the-ordinary state of affairs. They experience it as a normal and appropriate level of emotion.

Why We Love Emoters

Emoters are exciting and volatile. They show us how full of feeling life is and that emotional intensity is one of its beautiful experiences. By feeling so much about even simple or seemingly unimportant things, they give us a sense of the surprising and intricate complexity of life, the beauty of emotions, and the depth of feelings. They show us that emotional richness is one of the great untapped resources of our lives.

People who have suppressed their feelings, are out of touch with them, or were never permitted to develop the healthy expression of their emotions are often attracted to Emoters. That's because hysterical Emoters express feelings to such an exaggerated degree that the world of feelings becomes visible and real, often for the first time, to the person who has always avoided his or her emotions. Indeed, Emoters often express the feeling for both partners in a relationship, and this is their gift. They are doing the emoting for one or more people, so they often have to do it louder and more often than they would have to if the rest of us helped them out.

They are wonderful energy boosters, and so they're attractive to people who are depressed or lethargic. Emoters are a great antidote to low-energy or less intensely feeling types.

How They Drive Us Crazy

Emoters are a volcano of feelings that can erupt at any moment. You can always count on them to *feel* about something *and* to feel strongly. In addition, because their feelings are so intense, they always want to "process" everything so they can be relieved of the pressure of holding their intense emotions inside. What this usually means is that they want to tell you in no uncertain terms how bad everything felt to them, and they want you to either defend yourself, intricately understand their position, or beg for their forgiveness.

As a consequence, they're exhausting. They make relationships choppy and difficult. They make life jagged and fragmented. Sometimes they scare us. It's often scary being in the presence of such intense emotions, especially when they're directed at us. We don't know what to do. We feel out of our depth. We feel powerless. It takes a lot of energy to go through emotions at this level of intensity. Emoters wear us out because we don't like to live at these extremes. We don't like to live with the heat turned up so high that the pot is always boiling.

Additionally, Emoters can turn even the most placid, even-tempered, well-meaning person into an Emoter in their own right for minutes, hours, or a lifetime because they insist on engaging in the emotional realm at such a fevered pitch. This can make most other types want to run for cover.

What's Really Going On?

Emoters usually grew up in an environment that contained some form of hysteria as a constant, and as a result, excessive feeling excessively expressed is the only thing they recognize as a loving encounter. When the emotional level is finally all out and high-pitched, these people believe they're engaged in a real experience with another person. Anything short of this passionate encounter is passé. And so, whether things are calm or deserving of a major reaction, Emoters tend to do things that bring the relationship up to this high-pitched level of exchange. Then when both people are finally involved at a level of intensity that seems to the rest of us to be far above normal, the Emoter is finally happy. She feels as if at last she's connected with another person, and this passionate encounter is what she considers to be the true and appropriate form of engagement in relationship.

For example, Paul, who was often accused by his best friends of being the most emotional man on the planet, grew up in a family of twelve children with an alcoholic father who was overworked and beset by bills and the mayhem of having such a large family. Night after night he would come home drunk, and on a whim, or at the instruction of his wife, regularly beat up on the children. Whether or not a particular child was "due for a beating," they all lived in terror that this raving giant would come home and pulverize them. There was never a day of peace and tranquility in Paul's house. And there was no consistency except the routine of his father's getting drunk and, sure as shooting, beating up on somebody when he reached his alcohol limit.

Sheryl also grew up in a family that had hysterical overtones. It wasn't as obvious as an alcoholic father regularly beating his children, but her mother had a form of body hysteria which kept everybody in a state of panic. She worried constantly about germs. When the children went to a classmate's party, she would insist that all their underwear be soaked in Clorox for two or three days beforehand so they would be "protected from strange germs." Whenever Sheryl's mother or any of her children had a bug bite, scratch, scraped knee, or earache, she would catastrophize the worst and announce that this was the single incident in human history where a hangnail could lead to death.

Sheryl's mother kept everything in an uproar. No matter how minor the physical insult or injury, she would carry on about it, on the one hand worrying about her children and on the other making them feel that catastrophe was so commonplace that it was the only normal way to respond.

Now, both Paul and Sheryl are—you guessed it—Emoters in relationships. Although they don't express their hysteria in the same way that either of their parents did—Paul's a screamer and Sheryl's a thrower—both of them have short emotional fuses and can easily raise their voices to decibels that rock the neighborhood.

The Emoter's emotional wound is living in emotional chaos, and their response is either conscious or unconscious fear. Like Paul and Sheryl, most Emoters grew up in an environment where they were constantly terrorized and in which, therefore, *fear was the correct and appropriate emotional response.* The Emoter's childhood experience isn't that once in a while there's something to be afraid of. It is that every day is lived in a state of panic—with a schizophrenic mother, a sexually abusive uncle, a household that's an emotional war zone, to name just a few of the terrifying situations that breed adult Emoters. Such nonstop panic is an unnatural state, and the human body responds to this unending sense of fright by living in a heightened state of the flight or fight response.

What this means is that even as young children, Emoters are always prepared either to run away or fight back (yell, scream, throw things)—whatever it takes to secure their continued survival. Because they lived in this state throughout childhood, their reactions are also equally ingrained. It's very sad, but this heightened fight for survival has been the only consistent part of their life experience. They have lived in a state of fear for so long that they really don't know how not to. Everything that happens, no matter how small, is seen through the eyes of this desperate fear and fight for survival.

As a consequence, their tragedy is that they were deprived of the healing beauty of calm. They've never had the privilege of learning that interchanges of calm and depth, containing emotions as well as blurting them out, can have just as much meaning in a relationship as the all-out "expressing of feelings." In short, Emoters can't tell the difference between a meadow full of daisies and a roaring avalanche. Until the snow drifts are rolling down the side of the hill, burying people right and left, they don't think anything has happened. Thus, under the Emoter's excess of emotion is a profound longing for safety and peace.

The Difference Between an Emoter and Everyone Else

While the expression of intense emotion is an appropriate part of everyone's emotional repertoire, the Emoter carries it to extremes. Thus he sees all situations as worthy of excessive emotion and doesn't know how to evaluate when an intense emotional response is appropriate and when it could better be held at bay or saved for a more exciting occasion.

All of us have deep wells of feeling inside and intense experiences of loss, grief, excitement, and joy which can cause us to tap into our reservoirs of emotion and bring up feelings of great intensity. However, normal happy lovers will have discretion about when this intense emotion is appropriate and Emoters have little or no discretion.

Emoters also don't see their intensity as being intense. Because they lived their childhood in a metaphoric (or literal) madhouse, no matter how many decibels they're producing in getting their point across, they'll always tell you that they were just "telling you how they felt."

What Emoters Have to Teach Us

We live in a world that, paradoxically, has both over- and undervalued emotion. We see a dozen murders a day on TV and don't feel anything, even though it was once precisely our emotions that were meant to be aroused by such things. By living frequently in emotional excess, Emoters rekindle our awareness of the "good" and "bad" levels of feelings. They awaken our discernment. Looking at them, if we choose, we can take a stand about the appropriate and inappropriate uses of emotion in our relationships and in our culture.

Emoters also teach us about the beauty of emotional aliveness. In staying connected to their emotions, Emoters remind us that we all have an emotional essence, that there are things we should all feel deeply about. Until we do our share, they will continue to do the feeling for all the rest of us.

What Emoters Need to Learn About Relationships

The challenge for Emoters is to learn that there are other forms not only of love, but of emotional expression. That still waters also run deep. That we can feel intensely without making a scene and that sometimes the subtlety of emotions reaches deeper into our hearts than a sidewall crash in the stock car races at the Indianapolis Speedway.

Emoters need to learn that a relationship is a mixture of intense moments and plateaus of calm. In the quiescent periods of a relationship we are building depth simply by sharing experiences and companionship, learning the way each of us operates, enjoying the journey of the life we share. A walk on the beach, the delightful expressions of our children, our friendships and social life, movies, the news, the weather, the charcoal-broiled salmon you just fixed for dinner—all these are quiet notes that move us forward in the symphony of love. They are punctuated by the more dramatic moments and intensely expressed feelings that give a loud crescendo to its quiet forward movement.

And, while Emoters have a great deal to teach us about the depth and complexity of our emotional lives, how deep and important our feelings are, the irony is that they themselves often have a great deal to learn about emotions. How to moderate them, and how to express them appropriately, for example. In short, they need to learn that every relationship transgression isn't, in fact, a federal case.

In other words, Emoters need to learn that love is an inner as well as an outward process, that we can have strong feelings inside but not everything we feel inside has to be outwardly expressed. As they develop the capacity to hold and control their feelings, Emoters will discover that these unexpressed feelings can change them internally in a way that will make their relationship experiences much more comfortable and enjoyable.

At bottom, Emoters need to learn that the present is not the past, and that most likely, they are not in any kind of danger from the person with whom they are in relationship now. The more they can recognize their fear as a hangover from the past, the more they'll be able to let go of it and trust that whatever is going on at the moment can be addressed in a calm and yet feelingful manner.

What Emoters Can Do to Come Into Balance

1 Identify the form of hysteria in the household where you

grew up, and ask yourself to write about how you felt about it as a child.

Were you scared? Did it seem excessive? Were there times when you either tried or certainly believed that the person who was acting out terribly could have chosen another path?

As you go through this process of recollection, have compassion for yourself. Remember the child who was terrorized, beset, assaulted, dragged in and out of hoops, changability, and overreactiveness, and try to connect with how you wish your parents had responded in the situations that ignited their hysteria.

Take note, difficult though this may be, of how your own hysteria sometimes mimics that of your parents. Were they screamers, and are you one? Were they pot-throwers and have you, in your worst moments, become one? Do you raise your voice and scare people out of their wits just to get your point across the way your father or mother always did?

As you lovingly see the similarity, you will also create the possibility for change, especially as you remember the child who once knew that there must have been another way to handle things.

2 Breathe or meditate.

Some form of meditation or breath awareness is very beneficial for people who are overly emotional. This focusing of energy not only redistributes energy throughout the body, but gives you a time each day in which you experience the beauty of quiet and calm. Instead of reacting emotionally to every thought that comes by, you discover that many thoughts and perceptions that could be emotionally volatile to you in "normal waking hours" can, in a state of meditation, merely be observed.

This simple practice for twenty minutes a day or twenty minutes twice a day can take you a long way toward creating the awareness of another reality. When you see that there actually is another way to handle your emotions, you will more and more be able to deliver yourself and those you love from the uncontrollable outbursts that end up creating difficulties in your relationships, shattering intimacy, and causing you to feel embarrassed yourself.

3 Stop and ask yourself, What am I really afraid of?

Since the Emoter's driving emotion is fear, when you find yourself becoming hysterical about something—say, your wife hasn't been paying enough attention to you lately—ask yourself, What am I really afraid of? When you get to the bottom of your true fear—for example, that you're afraid your wife doesn't love you anymore, you can then have a talk with yourself (and your wife) about the real issue. Is your fear realistic? Or could there be something else going on? The more you get to your bottom-line fear, the less you will need to emote all over the person you love.

If you find this too hard to do on your own, ask your partner to ask you the question, "What are you really afraid of?" An Emoter I know, married to a Fantasizer, has him ask her this question anytime she feels herself getting really worked up. It works wonders in relieving her fear and bringing her back to earth.

4 Ask the other person what's going on.

After you've gained a little foothold in the world of calm, you can add another behavior that will also help you. The Emoter has biochemical, hair-trigger reactions to whatever precipitates his emotional response. Meditation, as I've already said, is helpful, as is figuring out what you're scared of. But another technique is this: instead of immediately reacting and assuming the worst, use the tried-and-true technique of simply asking other person what's going on. Did you really have the dog put to sleep this afternoon and is that why the food is still in his bowl, or is there some other reason I haven't suspected? Did you stand me up for a date because you're a thankless inconsiderate brute, or because you had a flat tire on the way to my house? Inquiry is very helpful in solving emotional problems.

The more you can calmly find out what was going on for the other person—she was planning to do it tomorrow, it was a special case that will never happen again, he was late because of stopping to buy you some flowers—the more you can see that whatever it was, it isn't worthy of an explosion.

5 Stop 86'ing your 10s.

One Emoter I know always used to do what I call "86'ing a 10." What I mean by this is that on a scale of 1 to 100, if a difficulty or a personal affront by a friend or a lover was actually about a 10 on the scale of 1 to 100—they were a few minutes late and forgot to call, they forgot the bread when they picked up the rest of the groceries, or they didn't mail the letter he'd asked them to mail that night but then remembered to mail the following morning—Harvey would "86 a 10." That is, for each of these minor relationship violations he would blow his stack halfway to kingdom-come, as if the violation were actually an 86 on a scale of 1 to 100.

Introducing realism into the Emoter's emotional vocabulary means realizing that a lot of things that go on in relationships, in fact the majority of them, are 3s, 5s, 10s, 12s, or 15s. Most of them are not 86s, or we wouldn't be in a relationship with that particular person in the first place. A nonstop 86 relationship wouldn't be worth having.

So, stop 86'ing your 10s and ask yourself, when something bugs you, where does it really fall on a scale of 1 to 100, and what, therefore, would be an appropriate emotional reaction to it.

6 Be willing to live in the calm.

As I've already pointed out, Emoters are so familiar with hysteria that to them it seems as if hysteria is what reality is made of. Just as a mouse might say that the moon is made of green cheese or a puppy might say that the whole world is filled with dog bones, so the Emoter would say that the whole world is hysterical—everything is always in a slightly chaotic state of upheaval that needs a similarly intense emotional response.

In order to modify your hysteria, you need to be willing to live in the calm. That means finding other satisfactions besides emotional intensity. Whether you're aware of it or not, emotional intensity actually creates an electrical charge in the body that's like a slight "high." It releases endorphins. That's why once you've delivered the feelings that may shatter the hearts or grey matter of your friends and lovers (leaving them to wonder if they ever again want to sit in that restaurant where you decided to scream your head off about the poor service), *you* will feel better. However, there are some other ways of handling things.

First of all, find other satisfactions in life. Develop a hobby. Do something that focuses your attention in a creative way so that the energy of your emotions can be directed toward something that will give you a specific, fruitful result instead of dispersing it through spontaneous, unbridled emotional expression.

Sean, an upholsterer who is overly emotional and always flying off the handle at his girlfriends, discovered in his forties that he had an unexpressed dimension as a creative artist. When he started painting, not only did his frustration with his paid vocation lessen, but he discovered that the focus required by his creativity actually melted his hysteria. The more he painted, the more he was able to get control of his feelings, and as time went on he was able to express them more and more appropriately in all of his relationships.

Emoters have a lot of energy that's looking for a channel. Find a hobby, a physical exercise, or a creative outlet that channels this energy, and it will bring emotional balance into your life.

7 Catch yourself and apologize.

Of course nobody's perfect, and you won't be either; and it would be boring if you could be. Not only that, but, as I've already pointed out, the rest of us need you to keep our own emotions ignited. But when you do go overboard and take it to the limit one more time, you can now catch yourself and apologize.

Sometimes there's such an unconscious embarrassment about hysterical behavior that rather than apologizing, we sort of slink off to a corner like the dog who messed the living room carpet and is trying to pretend it never happened. Instead of coming forward and making amends, Emoters often just disappear or go on to another random topic, like the weather: "Can you believe it's still raining?" "Gee, it's cold outside."

You can start changing if, each time you become aware of your behavior, you catch yourself and apologize. This will bring you calm and closeness and help you to appreciate the difference between inappropriate emotional behavior and emotions that are correct and worth expressing.

An apology doesn't take the difficult behavior away, but over time it gradually develops an inner awareness of the distinction between emotionally appropriate and hysterical behavior. Apologizing will allow you to see yourself as a person who can actually take control of your feelings, make them more appropriate to the situation, and feel less embarrassed in love.

A Meditation for Emoters

I don't have to be afraid any more. My fear used to be overwhelming, but the things that overwhelmed me are in the past. I don't have to yell. I can be heard when I whisper, if I quietly speak my truth. Love is the opposite of fear; the more I can let go of my fear, the more I can love and be loved.

Balancing Affirmations

I don't have to get upset about everything.

In a hundred years, what difference will it make?

I'm ready to give up being so afraid.

3

THE COOL CUCUMBER

"What, me worry?"

COOL CUCUMBERS ARE THE CALM, STEADY, OPTIMISTIC "even keelers" of the personality spectrum. They are reassuring to be around, because they're convinced that most everything will work out all right—so long as nobody gets too worked up about things. They are generally even-tempered, mild-mannered, and sunny-natured (until you present them with your feelings—and then they can go to great lengths to get away from you or to prevent you from expressing your emotions, especially sorrow or fear).

Cool Cucumbers tend to be methodical and are often slower-moving than other types. That's because their emotions never speed them up or carry them off. While Emoters can lift off like a rocket and carry you along with them, emotion-denying Cool Cucumbers tend to think that everything

61

falls in a pretty orderly pattern in a fairly reliable world. Since for them this is true, they also believe that you don't have to worry, or, if there's a problem, you can just "figure it out."

Ed and his wife Lorna were vacationing in Italy when over the news wire they heard of an earthquake in their hometown. Sixty people had died. Since they'd left their nine- and ten-year-old daughters at the home of friends near the announced epicenter of the earthquake, Lorna was understandably distraught.

When she urged Ed to call home (on phone lines that were repeatedly jammed), he minimized her concern. "What are the statistical chances that out of the sixty people who died, two of them could be our children?" he said.

Chagrined by his cavalier response, Lorna persisted until finally two days later, she was able to get through and be assured that, despite some damage to their neighborhood, the children were safe. "See, what did I tell you?" said Ed. "We could have saved the money for that overseas phone call and gone out to dinner."

Like other emotion-deniers, Ed looks at most of life from a practical point of view. Reason, logic, probability—these are the tools of the Cool Cucumber. Indeed, most Cool Cucumbers navigate through life via logic only, and distrust other people's feelings precisely because they're not logical. Other personality types, particularly Emoters and People Pleasers, are drawn to Cool Cucumbers because their steadiness levels out the ups and downs of their more intense, emotional lives.

Cool Cucumbers can be counted on to be the calm at the eye of the storm, the voice of reason, and no matter what your problem, they can probably offer you some sound practical advice.

Telltale Signs of a Cool Cucumber

- You are calm and collected, especially in a crisis.

- People are drawn to your steadiness and unflappability.

- You "never" cry.

- You argue with people when they suggest that you should be feeling something.

- You most always base your decisions on facts or logic.

- You want to be in control.

- You're convinced that what happened in your childhood is irrelevant to how you are now.

- Other people tell you that you're detached, remote, withdrawn, or just too practical.

A Closer Look: Distinguishing Characteristics of Cool Cucumbers

1 The Cool Cucumber doesn't believe in the reality of feelings.

The Cool Cucumber isn't aware that along with work, play, economic life, sunrise, and moonlight, life is also a river of feelings. To the Cool Cucumber, it's as if the world of emotion is something that somebody else invented and he or she enters it very reluctantly. Every once in awhile someone presents strong feelings to the Cool Cucumber, and this is an event that's difficult to deal with and is avoided as much as possible. It's as if the world of feelings just isn't in the Cool Cucumber's repertoire.

Because they're uncomfortable with feelings, they are also reluctant to acknowledge that events in the past could be having an emotional effect on them now. "Childhood? That happened a long time ago," the emotion-denying Cucumber may say to the lover, wife, or therapist who has the nerve to suggest that those beatings he got in childhood could have some effect on him now.

The Cool Cucumber doesn't understand that there is a continuous emotional thread in each of us that runs from childhood to adulthood and expresses itself most particularly in our intimate relationships. "What's the big deal?" the Cool Cucumber will say to the person whose feelings got hurt because of a coworker's put-down, or a best friend's nasty remark about her new boyfriend. "You only live once; enjoy it; don't dwell on your troubles."

For the Cool Cucumber, the glass is always half-full, even if it's leaking like a sieve at the bottom or it's only as big as a thimble. Basically the Cool Cucumber doesn't believe that the emotional world exists, and it often takes a gigantic upheaval for them to finally discover it in all its stunning, life-changing reality.

For many Cool Cucumbers, an unexpected divorce will be their first emotional awakening, the catalyst that propels them, against their will, into the world of their feelings. Interestingly enough, it's the catastrophes that Emoters always think are about to happen that are often the actual wake-up calls for Cool Cucumbers. Emotion-phobic Cucumbers would rather do almost anything than deal with their emotions.

2 The Cool Cucumber denies feelings—their own and yours.

In psychological terms, the Cool Cucumber's issue is denial and sublimation. *Sublimation* is a word psychologists use to explain how, below the level of consciousness, we divert our raw emotional energy into more socially acceptable behavior. For example, the girl who wants to scream and wail about how her father was off in the Saudi Arabian oilfields for eleven years, but instead throws herself into her schoolwork and becomes the head of her class, is "sublimating" the pain of his absence. Similarly, the boy who talks about how clean his mother always kept the house is "sublimating" the pain of never being held by her because she was always cleaning. Sublimation is the way Cool Cucumbers shove their emotions down.

Since on a conscious level the Cool Cucumber doesn't believe that the world of emotions exists, when their feelings do come up—they've just lost their job, their father died, their wife is threatening to leave them—they just deny the reality of their feelings in all these matters. "Oh, it's not so bad. We're just having a bad fight. She'll get over it; it's PMS." Or, "No big deal. There's more work where that came from." Or, "I don't know why you have to get so upset. Everyone dies. That's part of life. Why should I be sad?"

Not only do Cool Cucumbers deny their feelings, they also conduct a subtle (and often not-so-subtle) campaign to deny anybody else's right to feel. For example, Laurel had planned a much-needed vacation. A busy elementary school teacher, she was overly exhausted because her aging father had Alzheimer's, and, along with her teaching, she spent a great deal of time looking after him. After negotiating with her live-in lover, Jeff, to take a trip to Bali, she was looking forward to her time of rejuvenation.

While she was rushing to pack, her father had an episode that required some extra attention, and when she finally got to the airport ninety miles away, she discovered that she had forgotten her passport. Tearful and angry at herself, she drove home and showed up weeping at the door, where Jeff, a classic Cucumber, was watching Monday night football. When she blurted out what had happened, crying all the while, Jeff just said, "Don't be so upset. It's no big deal." And when she added, plaintively, "But I've missed a whole day of my vacation," he added, "Well, that's no big deal either. You can go tomorrow." Instead of empathizing with Laurel, Jeff discounted her feelings and practically made her feel like a fool for being upset in the first place.

Cool Cucumbers are notorious for trying to keep emotions to a minimum, vigilant about making sure that nothing so wild and woolly as a raw emotion could interrupt the supposed calm of their relationships—or their own lives.

3 The Cool Cucumber is fact-oriented, basing decisions on logic.

The Cool Cucumber is mentally focused. Since the Cool Cucumber lives in a world in which there are no feelings, he or she makes all his decisions, even in feeling matters, on logic or intelligence. The Cool Cucumber is very thorough, often conducting research on a given item, such as whether he should marry a particular person or have a baby, which are ultimately emotional choices, as if he were writing a Ph.D. dissertation or a consumer's report. Instead of including their feelings, they're certain that the results of their research will be an adequate basis for a decision.

A skillful young woman lawyer I know, continually amused and somewhat irritated by the endless emotional peregrinations of her mother, would often say to her at point-blank range, "What's so hard about making a decision? Just look at the facts and then make up your mind." Sometimes she would gather data in an effort to assist. "This one's less expensive than that one, so why not buy the cheap one?" she'd suggest. Because her mother could never make a decision based on just the data, her daughter would become frustrated and eventually give up. Later she'd be amazed when her mother did make a decision, based, as she saw it, "on nothing at all."

A successful young businessman, trying to buy his first home, spent a year and a half looking at properties in all types of areas. When friends asked him why this process was so tedious and time-consuming he said repeatedly, "I have to analyze all the variables." He failed to take into consideration that some areas and houses were actually more pleasing to him than others. Having analyzed all the properties from only the financial perspective, he concluded that a property some distance out of town would be the "best investment." Satisfied by his research he purchased it. But within two months he found that all the things about it that actually (unbeknownst to him) affected him emotionally were of far greater importance than he had ever imagined. It was too far from town; it was in a dark valley and he never saw the sunlight; all the things he liked to do were now forty-five minutes away. Within two months he put it up for sale and sold it. He was finally able to tell himself that it just didn't "feel quite right up there." Basing his decision on logic alone, he lost $30,000.

Laurie, a young hospital administrator, moved from town to town in her quest for higher and higher salaries. She left a boyfriend behind wherever she went. She did this because "the most important thing" to her was her career. Her father had never made enough money; she was going to be sure that she did. Finances had always been a sore point in her parents' relationship, and she didn't want to repeat the pattern they had set up.

Not realizing that this was really an emotion-driven goal (avoiding the mistakes of her parents), Laurie kept believing that each time her decision was based only on money and that objective financial reality was all that really mattered to her. Interestingly enough, because of her endless financial analyses, rather than having a marriage troubled with discontents over money, Laurie had no relationship at all.

4 Cool Cucumbers don't take into account that their actions in relationships will have an emotional effect on the other person.

Brent, in a relationship with Liz for more than two years, couldn't understand why Liz blew up when he unilaterally decided to take a hiking vacation with his two buddies from work. One Friday, when they were out for a romantic dinner, he just announced that he and Scott and Tom were taking off to Yosemite for two weeks.

When Liz reacted, he responded by giving her a long list of all the reasons why he needed a vacation. He didn't take into consideration the fact that they'd been dating for two years and that she might want to go on a vacation with him. It was only when, in utter frustration, she threatened to break up with him that he tumbled to the fact that his actions could have an effect on her feelings.

Dennis, a successful Web site designer, was always late coming home. He always had a reason. Forty-five minutes to two hours after he was expected, he'd come rolling in, a smile on his face, and put his arms around Lisa, who was invariably fuming. "Why are you so upset?" he'd ask, as if her reaction was uncalled for. When she explained that she was irritated, scared, or angry, he'd brush her off. "I'm home now," he'd say. "What's the big deal?" And if she persisted in trying to explain her position, he'd treat her as if she were a total fool, and accuse her of grossly overreacting.

Because of the Cool Cucumber's consistent avoidance of emotion, people get angry at Cool Cucumbers and often end up blowing up, walking out, or divorcing them after a lengthy marriage which the Cucumbers themselves thought was happy. "I've been happy all this time. I don't know why you haven't been," they often say to spouses packing their suitcases and walking out the front door. Their lovers and partners often become overly emotional, expressing for both partners the feelings that Cool Cucumbers deny.

Why We Love Cool Cucumbers

Cool Cucumbers are the steady-as-she-goes ballast of the love types. They hold the line, hold the fort, keep the world fixed, fastened, repaired, running on schedule, and moving along without too many interruptions or upheavals. We count on them *precisely to be unemotional* at times of great emotion. They are the ones who play the last song when *Titanic* goes down, who walk into the fire to carry the children out of the burning house, who stop and change the tire of a stranger at the side of the road without worrying about the potentially dangerous consequences to themselves, simply because it's a problem that needs to be solved. They know that life is about what needs to be done—you just figure it out and then do it. They are reliable and steady. We can always count on them. The rest of us are grateful—when we're going through our emotional upheavals—that they do hold the compass and raise the red flag in the middle of the swamp, or remain unmovable and unaffected in times of disaster.

These unemotional types make great husbands, wives, and business partners. They take responsibility seriously. They fulfill it like clockwork. They can be counted upon. They're usually not complainers, because since they don't recognize their feelings, they usually don't think that anything's worth complaining about. They are the bulwarks of humanity and the steady keel of any intimate relationship.

How They Drive Us Crazy

Sweethearts, lovers, and spouses have trouble with Cool Cucumbers because you can never really get close to them. They don't want to "dwell" on things. They never just tumble into their feelings and exult in the pleasures of the emotional world. As a consequence, you never get to have the kind of exquisitely intimate relationship that only a two-way exchange of deep feelings can offer. Those in relationship with them often describe them as detached, remote, or withdrawn.

Although every other type can drive you crazy, Cool Cucumbers have a special talent for crazy-making. That's because their essence is to deny not only their own feelings but yours as well. In this emotionally unreal world they leave their partners feeling odd and off-key for having feelings in the first place and expressing them in the second.

While Cool Cucumbers usually choose people who are in touch with their feelings as their partners—to make up for their own imbalance—they often launch an unconscious campaign to keep their partners from letting any feelings out of the bag, as if emotions were like wild cats, dangerous when let loose. In their across-the-board denial of the emotional dimension of human experience, they unconsciously cause the people who love them to gradually suppress their feelings until at some point all these suppressed feelings often lead to an explosion.

Another reason spouses and lovers grow weary of them is that they tend to be joy stealers. By reducing everything to a reason, a practical outlook, a logical conclusion, or an analysis of the variables, they can take the sunshine out of the summer day, the spontaneity out of the birthday party, and the romance out of a love affair. They'll buy the smallest diamond possible for your engagement ring because it was "a good buy," take you on a bargain vacation because "it was a great package deal," and not jump up and down for joy when you plan a surprise fortieth birthday party for them, because "being forty is no big deal." Instead of being touched, overjoyed, or deeply moved by anything—thereby forging a precious emotional bond—they'll as likely say, when you ask them if they liked the party, "Yeah, I had a nice time."

What's Really Going On?

Underneath all their logic and practicality, *Cool Cucumbers struggle with the emotional wound of sorrow;* their form of coping is denial. In the life of every Cool Cucumber there is some very painful thing that they had to deny: the pain of adoption, the heart hurt of living with a cool, ignoring parent, the sorrow of being a child of divorce.

In order to cope with their pain, Cool Cucumbers learned early on to deny their emotions. As a consequence, they truly do not know *how* to gain access to them. Although all their feelings are down there, locked in a dark sub-basement of their psyche, the Cool Cucumber can't turn on the light and find his way down the stairs. Sometimes their sorrow is profound, like the loss of a parent by death. And sometimes it's the quiet, continuous emotional coolness of a parent that slowly breaks their heart.

Walt, breaking down after years of therapy, said it was simply that he could *never* get his mother's attention. He loved her, but she was always busy with some interior decorating project. She never held him, never read to him, never kissed him good-night. One day he came home with his knee sliced up from a bicycle accident. It was bleeding badly as he walked into the kitchen and all she said was, "Don't get blood all over the floor."

"That's when I shut down," Walt recalled. "That was the day, the minute, the hour."

Wilfred, another Cool Cucumber, was one of four boys whose father died of a protracted case of tuberculosis when Wilfred was three. Overwhelmed by her widowhood and the burden of her four young sons, his mother sought very quickly to marry again. She did this, and promptly produced three more children, so that within a period of a just a few years, Wilfred and his original siblings found themselves in a family of seven. Not wanting to disrupt the flow of her newly knitted-together family, Wilfred's mother behaved as if everything was hunky-dory. All seven children now had a father, and family life resumed with hardly a crinkle or crease.

While on the surface all seemed to be well and, in fact, the family prospered in all the usual ways, Wilfred's tremendous feelings of loss remained stifled and suppressed. Wilfred and his brothers had experienced one of the most devastating losses a child can experience, the death of their father, and yet this loss had been denied, basically shoved under the rug. They had never had a chance to grieve. Indeed, once she was married again, Wilfred's mother never again spoke of Wilfred's father. It was as if he had evaporated into thin air, or perhaps even more, as if he'd never existed and was only a figment of their imagination.

The children's appropriate sorrow was never permitted room or time. Wilfred's mother kept reminding them how lucky and happy they were. "Don't we have a great family?" she would always say. "Aren't we having a wonderful time?" Since Wilfred had experienced the greatest loss any child can endure, and since his emotions had been totally denied, he grew up, of course, to be a Cool Cucumber. After that, nothing in his life seemed worthy of an emotional response; the one huge event that deserved it had been treated as if it had never happened.

Wilfred is a first-class emotion-denier. When asked how he is, he always says, "I'm perfect." He's had several relationships, all of which came to an end because he ignored the feelings of his girlfriends. He's also been engaged a couple of times, but when one fiancée's mother was in a serious car accident and he refused to accompany his girlfriend to the hospital (where her mother died a few days later), she broke up with him. A second engagement was broken when, after a year of trying every which way to get Wilfred to express his feelings, his fiancée just gave up.

Like the death of a parent, divorce is another experience through which children learn to deny their feelings. Because divorce has become by now almost an American institution, the feelings that naturally accompany it are all the more easily denied.

Parents tend to see the end of a marriage as a loss and failure of their own, while giving only passing attention to the emotional issues that are surfacing for their children. Children are assumed to be able to handle the burgeoning array of stepparents, stepsiblings, and shuttling back and forth between households that are the unavoidable consequences of divorce, without having any feelings about it.

It isn't that children don't, in fact, have to adjust to these new circumstances, it's that so often we deny the depth or complexity of feelings that goes along with this emotionally devastating event. We don't leave room for the feelings or take them seriously enough, and so children of divorce, too, often grow up to become Cool Cucumbers.

For example, Holly's parents were divorced when she was six. One day she came home from school and her father told her he was moving out because "her mother didn't love him anymore." He moved downtown, and, although he saw Holly every weekend, he never discussed the matter again, while Holly's mother, feeling guilty about initiating the divorce, tried to focus on the positive by supporting Holly in school and all her extracurricular undertakings.

Not long after, Holly's father met a new woman and started living with her. Holly's world now included a part-time stepmother who wasn't particularly fond of her, but nobody talked about that either. A few months later her father and his girlfriend moved across the country and, after they were secretly married, invited Holly to visit for the summer.

Meanwhile, back home, Holly's mother had a string of boyfriends, all of whom liked Holly but disappeared just at the point Holly seemed to make a connection with them.

A few years later, Holly's father moved back across the country to take a new job, bringing his wife and their new son along. His new family settled not far away from Holly and her mother and immediately expected Holly to fit in with them. She did, as best she could, until several years later her father moved "up North" because her stepmother wanted "their own family." Once there, Holly's father virtually forgot about her, never called or wrote, and even stopped sending child support.

Holly, a basically sunny-natured person, took all this in stride—or so it seemed. An emotionally Cool Cucumber, she has enjoyed success in various areas, school, work, and even friendships, as if this variegated life, repetitive of the fragmentation of her childhood, were the norm. Eventually Holly married, an unemotional bond—"He liked dogs and so did I; we both wanted to buy a house"—and it was only when this marriage ended because her husband accepted a job in New Zealand and she didn't want to go that she started having the anxiety attacks that set her on the journey of getting in touch with her emotions.

It isn't only situations in which feelings are denied that can create the suppression of feelings in adults. Sometimes it's the opposite—overly hysterical parents, households so out of control emotionally that they cause children to make an unconscious decision not to feel. It's almost as if the emotional experience of an entire lifetime has already occurred and, in desperation, the child says, "I will never feel, I'll never go down that road again. I've handled too many emotions already. I can't stand anymore—mine or anyone else's."

Cool Cucumbers are often very sensitive people whose own profound sensitivity has been locked away because they don't know how to find the key to it. Either that, or they wonder if they could survive actually going through the feelings that might surface if they ever got in touch with them. Rather than dealing with their emotional experiences one by one, a single step at a time, as would be the case in the normal course of emotional development, for the Cool Cucumber the original devastating events have become so submerged that the feelings that would come up around them would be commensurately gigantic.

Cool Cucumbers need to be treated with the compassion appropriate to the deep wounds they have experienced and gently drawn out of the cave of their apparent inability to feel. Above all, they need to reconnect with their sorrow, the painful loss, or continuing deprivation that once broke their hearts. They also need to cry. The tears they've suppressed will carry them gradually to the river of their own feelings.

The Difference Between a Cool Cucumber and Everyone Else

As we've learned from looking at Emoters, there's a balance that needs to be achieved in all our emotional lives. Excess in either direction upsets the grace of living. There are times when the suppression of emotions is not only necessary but appropriate. Most of us know that there are times to hold back feelings—when you're comforting someone else, for example, so they can shed their tears and work through their feelings without you sitting down beside them and have a bawling fit of your own. Indeed, when someone else is going through his or her grief or having a difficult day and you have taken on the role of the listener, it's appropriate to keep your feelings about your own lousy, rotten day to yourself. Most of us know how to move through the rhythms of suppressing and expressing our feelings and have an appropriate map of when which is legitimate.

Cool Cucumbers, however, suppress feelings to such a degree that even when their own health or well-being might depend on the expression of a feeling, they can't call it up.

For example, I know a young man whose twin brother was killed in a car accident coming home from college for Christmas vacation. Vern was supposed to have traveled in the same car with his brother, but because of a belated exam, flew home several days later. He had shared an enjoyable childhood with Clyde but later watched as his brother went through the high school years with academic difficulties and problems with drugs.

Unbeknownst to Vern, he felt guilty about Clyde's troubled past because they were twins. Although he couldn't admit it to himself, he couldn't understand why Clyde's path had been consistently more difficult than his. Being a Cool Cucumber, he went to his brother's funeral without shedding a tear, stood in a daze while people offered condolences, and later, when asked about Clyde's death, said that it "really hadn't affected him much."

Obviously Vern had suffered a great loss, one worthy of having deep feelings about. But he claimed not to feel much. As this story shows, the difference between Cool Cucumbers and everyone else is that the rest of us know when it's appropriate to suppress our emotions and Cool Cucumbers don't.

Cool Cucumbers would deny that they're upset about being identified as an Emotion Denier. "What's the big deal?" they'd say. "It's not a problem." They're so out of touch with the world of emotions that it doesn't even exist to them as something they've been cut off from.

What Cool Cucumbers Have to Teach Us

Cool Cucumbers remind us that our feelings aren't the only thing that matters in any given situation. They also offer the positive perspective that indeed, things usually do turn out all right, even if at any given moment it seems like they're totally falling apart. For all the things that go wrong in the world, all the things that we can get upset about, these steadfast optimists—precisely because of their denial—can keep us in touch with the basic goodness of life. They teach us, also, about the simple beauty of shouldering our burdens, getting the job done without muss or fuss, carrying on.

What Cool Cucumbers Need to Learn About Relationships

Cool Cucumbers need to see that the richness of any relationship abides precisely in the exchange of feelings. It's how we feel about one another and the continual pleasing expression of our feelings of care and affection, of empathy, delight, hurt, joy, passion, interest, and great pleasure in one another that gives a relationship its true richness. No two people ever stayed happy because they were always analyzing what was going on, or because they'd reached the bottom line of all the variables and made a rational decision. Happiness in the relationship realm comes because we continually delight one another with the small, ever-changing pleasures of just telling each other who we are and what we feel at any given moment.

More than anything else, relationships are this emotional interchange. When the exchange of feelings is wonderful in a relationship, we're happy to be there. When we stop enjoying exchanging our feelings, the relationship doesn't "feel good" anymore, and that's when we head for the door.

What Cool Cucumbers Can Do to Come Into Balance

Since the problem of Cool Cucumbers is that they don't know how to gain access to their feelings, most of the remedies for this personality type are actual exercises to increase feeling capacity.

1 Get acquainted with the four winds of feeling.

The emotional basics are that we all have four general areas of feeling: joy, sorrow, fear, and anger. It doesn't matter who you are, where you came from, whether your parents denied or expressed their feelings or whether you do or don't—there are still four quadrants, or as I call them, "four winds of feeling," that are part of the human emotional repertoire.

The first thing Cool Cucumbers need to do is "get it" that, just like everybody else, whether they know it or not, experience it or not, or believe it or not, they too are blown by the four winds of feelings. Here's a practice exercise to begin this acquaintance with your feelings. Either at the beginning or the end of each day, ask yourself the following questions:

What am I sad about?

What am I happy about?

What am I angry about?

What am I scared of?

Try hard to identify something in your current life that belongs in each of these quadrants. For example, "I'm scared I got sunburned. I'm happy I'm on vacation. I'm angry I got awakened by that 5:00 A.M. wrong number phone call. I'm sad that my sweetheart couldn't come to this party with me."

As you gradually go through these exercises, you will discover that you are a feeling person. No matter how minimal your feelings may seem, they nevertheless point to the direction in which bigger feelings about the bigger events of your life reside: losses or joys that have been turning points in your personal history—the day you won your varsity letter, the day you finally quit smoking, the night you met your wife at that party, the devastating panic when you learned your mother was dying.

2 Ask yourself where in your body you *feel* something and assign an emotion to it.

For example, do you have an aching back? A stiff neck? Do your feet hurt? Locate this pain. Write down where it is, and then pretend that each of these physical pains actually represents an emotion. Is your aching back your anger at your boss? Is that pain in your neck your irritation with your secretary? Do your feet hurt because you feel like you just can't stand up another day behind the cash register at the store, because you want to run away, or because you feel ungrounded, out of touch with your values? Is that pain in your chest a heartache about the canceled date last Friday night?

More and more we are learning that all our emotions take residence in our body. They're not just ideas in our mind or notions that vaguely pass through our consciousness. They actually express themselves in our cells, tissues, and organs. What are the pains, discomforts, slight irritations, or outright physical agonies that you are suffering from right now? What are they telling you about your emotions, the way you really feel about things?

3 Remember sad and happy things from childhood.

Although the four quadrants of feelings are operating at all times, the things that brought us the most joy or the most pointed sorrow are the most significant lodestars for our emotions. So, stop now and take the time to identify your most painful memory from childhood. What happened? Who was involved in the situation? How did it affect you then? How do you suppose it affects you now? (No, you can't say it's not affecting you now. See if you can come up with some awareness of a connection between that event and some current feeling.)

For example, Lon said, "It was the death of my dog Rusty, who got run over in the street in front of our house. On my way home from school I saw a car pulled off to the side of the road and him lying bloody in front of the house. My mom was inside busy talking on the phone and she didn't seem to get what a big deal it was. She just kept talking. My dad came home a few minutes later. When she told him what had happened he walked out to the street with me. Then, he just picked up Rusty's body and put it in a burlap bag and never asked me how I felt. They were busy planning a trip, and my dad just said, 'Well, he was old anyway.'

"Since my dad didn't think Rusty's death was worth crying about, I guess I decided it wasn't either. I thought my dad knew best. I followed in his footsteps. And became an emotion-denier. A man."

Conversely, what's a happy moment you remember from childhood? Susie says her happiest memory is when she won a camera at the school fair. Susie's family was poor and she had always felt very unlucky. It was painfully obvious that all the other kids in her class had more money and more things than she did. They always had pretty clothes and got great presents at their birthday parties.

"I was beginning to feel like I was just an unlucky person, sort of doomed," Susie said. "And then, when I was in third grade I won this automatic camera at the carnival at school. I wasn't even particularly interested in cameras, but just the fact that I won it made me really happy. I felt like the course of my life had changed. I went out the very next day and bought some film, which took just about all the baby-sitting money I'd saved up, but I decided to go for it. When I took my first pictures and saw how they came out, I felt like I had a connection to the world that I'd never had before. That camera changed my life. It gave me a new way to relate to people and things. It made me feel lucky, like I could have friends, and it gave me my first feelings of security. I'm able to be a photojournalist today because of the confidence I gained through that experience."

4 Ask yourself, What would logic do? What would feeling do?

Give yourself an emotional comparison task. Take a current situation in your life about which you have to make a decision and ask yourself, What would logic do? and What would feeling do? It can be any decision, no matter how small. (In fact, a small one would be good to start with.)

For example, Victor and Linda were out buying pillows for their new bed and looked at a lot of pillows at the white sale. Linda liked the down pillows because they were soft and squishy. She felt like they would hug up on her head more at night. But when Victor looked at the prices, he saw that the pillows that were combined feather and down had been marked down a greater percentage than the down-only pillows, even though both were on sale.

"Well that's it. Let's get the down-and-feather pillows," Victor said. "They're marked down 40 percent and the pure down pillows are only marked down 20 percent."

Linda was about to succumb to his unemotional analysis of the pillow issue when she suggested that he lay his head on one of the pillows and see how it actually felt. The minute he did, he saw that it felt wonderful, and even though he had a struggle passing up the higher discount, Linda finally talked him into it.

What are the decisions you're making in your life right now? If it's to buy a house, for example, are you going to choose the "best deal" or the one that has a certain emotional quality—a quiet street, a beautiful garden—that will make you feel at home? Is it because it's in the right part of town, or when you think of waking up there in the morning you know that it will really make you happy? Notice how hard it is to "go with your feelings," and since you're as logic-oriented as you probably are, make a list of the specific rewards you would receive if you went with your feelings instead of your reasoning this time around.

5 Let others teach you about feelings.

Another good exercise is to ask other people how they feel. For example, if you're buying a house, ask people, "How do you feel about your house? Why did you choose it?" Notice the kind of responses people who are in touch with their feelings generally give; they can be your teachers.

For example, when Molly was trying to by a house, she asked all her friends why they bought theirs. "I like the way the light comes in the windows in the morning," one said. Another said, "The people next door have a beautiful swimming pool and just looking at it makes me feel peaceful." And a third said, "I know this is the kind of house where my grandchildren will love to come and play."

Whatever the issue you're trying to solve, collect a number of responses from a variety of people so you begin to see how your feelings might guide you in the decision you're trying to make.

6 Do something emotionally daring.

Being a Cool Cucumber means living with feelings held in by barriers that have been put up over many years and with a great deal of care. Whittling away or blasting through these barriers will allow you to experience your emotional self. Don't wait for a personal, emotional tragedy to teach you. Start being a risk taker now. Do something where you can have an experience of losing control, that is, of not doing it "the way you've always done it" and discover the feelings that come up around this changed behavior.

Try exploring your own emotional life and allow the way you feel about things to be a part of the experience you share with the person you love, even if it feels stupid or scary. Go bungee jumping. Go rope swinging over a mountain lake. Answer a personals ad, despite how weird you think they are or the fact that you swore you'd never do that. Take a class in self-defense if you're a woman, or ballet dancing if you're a man. Long and short of it, break your pattern.

This is important because when you do something different, you break up deeply entrenched patterns of behavior. These patterns actually form pathways in our brains where our neurons learn to fire in a certain way and become gradually incapable of firing in other ways. What this means, simply, is that we all get in ruts of thinking and behaving that are very hard to break out of. As Will Rogers said, "Choose your ruts carefully. You're going to be in them for a long, long time."

Basically, changing your behavior and doing something unexpected, something uncharacteristic for you, will create little doorways, pathways, and openings in which you can be caught off-guard by your emotions and begin the journey of discovering the pleasures and the challenges of your emotional life.

A Meditation for Cool Cucumbers

Deep down, I am a man/woman of sorrows. These sorrows have shaped me and are precious. I want to feel them now and let them take me. To my joys, to love. To the peace that comes from living from both my feelings and my logic at once.

Balancing Affirmations

Yes, I do have feelings. Yes, feelings are real.

I can feel without losing control or access to my logical mind.

Loving is about feeling. I want to love and I want to feel.

THE SKEPTIC

"Love? Where's my bazooka!?"

SKEPTICS ARE THE PEOPLE WHO SOMEHOW NEVER have a relationship—or, if they do, not for long. Many Skeptics claim flat out that they don't believe in love; others just somehow never seem to find the right person or have given up all hope of finding a good relationship. When they do get into a relationship, something invariably goes wrong, so that, once again, they end up alone. They frequently have jobs that greatly impede the possibility of a long-term relationship: they're traveling salespeople or merchant marines; they work on an oil rig, or they've taken a design job that requires relocating to Asia for six months.

Skeptics tend to be very funny, and often have a dark, sardonic sense of humor. They can always look on the bleak side of things, but in such a way that tends to be very amusing to everyone around them. Irony and pessimism are the tools of their trade: the bumper sticker "Life's a bitch and then you die" pretty much sums up their worldview. Often the butt of their humor is themselves. The Skeptic brother of one of my friends always calls up and identifies himself as "your scumbag brother," and a female Skeptic I know always says, "Who'd want to go out with me? I look like the Witch of Endor."

Skeptics are right out front with their negativity about relationships, but deep down they really would like to fall in love and have their skepticism bashed to bits by the miracle they thought could never occur.

Rodney is a classic Skeptic. Intelligent, charming, and witty, he got married right out of college to a woman he didn't love because he was so sure that love didn't exist. He knew he wanted to have kids and so did she; that's why he married her. After a few years and two children, the impossible happened—he fell in love with Jane, a vivacious, intelligent young woman he met at work. Swept away by feelings he thought he would never experience, he left his wife to go live with Jane. At first, life was blissful for Rodney as he basked in feelings of love that he had never felt before. But as time went on, the feelings wore off and day-to-day reality set in. Besides, Jane wanted a real relationship and soon ended up "nagging" Rodney about spending more time and having a deeper connection with him. Tiring of these "arguments," as he called them, Rodney decided that he'd been right in the first place. He left Jane, telling everyone that "there's no such thing as love," and now contents himself with short-term affairs.

Telltale Signs of a Skeptic

- You are clever and witty, and often make fun of yourself.

- Often self-deprecating, you have a cynical worldview.

- You don't really believe that love exists.

- You have created an independent life for yourself that satisfies you.

- You prefer the status quo to change.

- You have a difficult time being around people who are expressing their emotions.

A Closer Look: Distinguishing Characteristics of Skeptics

1 Skeptics have a consistently negative worldview.

You can always tell a Skeptic because he or she will always tell you how bad things are or were. Nothing is likely to get better either. Although, as we've already said, they can be lighthearted about this miserable state of affairs, this is consistently—and really—the way they look at life.

2 Skeptics are incredibly ambivalent about relationships.

Skeptics' usual PR about relationships is that they want one, but at the same time they're always telling you that "there are no good men left," "there's no such thing as love," or "it'll never work out anyway and so why even bother." Just the same, they take many of the actions others take when they're looking for love: they're lurking in yoga classes, going on hikes, occasionally even trying a computer dating service. That's because, although they say they don't believe in love, there's a little tiny part of them that does, or that hopes against hope that somehow they'll be proven wrong.

But just to protect their skepticism, they arrange their lives in such a way that it's virtually impossible that they could ever be proven wrong.

Jill, a Skeptic acquaintance of mine, typifies this ambivalence. She's had two simultaneous twenty-year relationships, both with married men. She sees each of them once every couple of months. The fact that they're both married ensures that they won't spend too much time with her or get too close emotionally. At the same time, she tells all her friends that she's looking for a more committed relationship—that what she really wants is a husband—but in actuality, her involvement with these two men prevents her from truly being available to anyone else. So although she looks half-heartedly, and occasionally even lets friends fix her up, her life is really too full for a serious relationship.

As this story shows, Skeptics have high-voltage ambivalence. It's not just the usual seesaw of Do I want a relationship now or later, or Do I want it with this one or that one? Their ambivalence draws from the farthest, most extreme ends of the spectrum: I want a relationship, but I really don't believe it's possible, so only if you bang me on the head, drag me off, and make it happen will I go along.

This ambivalence is hard on Skeptics—and on everyone else. Even though they're practically almost 100 percent settled into the giving up mode, they still, somewhere inside, hold out the hope against hope that someone, somehow, sometime will prove them totally wrong.

3 To the extent that they do believe in love, Skeptics deny love more than they deny their skepticism.

Even though in reality, the chances of a good thing happening are just about equal to those of a bad or really terrible thing happening, the Skeptic hedges his bets, where love is concerned, on the side of disappointment and discontent. "It'll never work out anyway, so why should I go on that blind date?" "Of course they got divorced—how else does a love story end?"

Basically Skeptics have lost their willingness to take an emotional risk—they're not willing to chance that they really might fall in love, that it could actually be wonderful, that they could learn to enjoy it. As a consequence, if they do get into a relationship, it's always with something held back—the total emotional vulnerability that falling in love really is.

The truth is, love can't give all its wonders and pleasures to the person who is rapping his knuckles on the table and saying, "Show me!" Love only comes through for people who dive in.

4 Skeptics sabotage the relationships they do have.

Sometimes, because of that teeny-weeny little part of them that really does want to fall in love, the Skeptic stumbles, or, once in a while, even dives headlong into a relationship. The man I know who said "Love? Where's my bazooka!?" did this, in fact. After being skeptical for years, he finally melted a little—"I've been alone too long; I'm too set in my ways. I think I'll give love a try," he said. Then, he took the leap and got into a relationship. He acknowledged that it was a leap and even openly begged the woman who fell in love with him to help him open his heart. But an open heart was scary to him—he'd have to deal with all the things that had made him a Skeptic in the first place—and when he saw that love was going to take work, he started backpedaling like crazy. A couple of months down the road, he decided he "just had to" take the job that moved him a couple of thousand miles away.

This is a typical pattern for the Skeptic. Try—and then give up. Even when they've surrendered into a relationship, they're looking for ways to escape—whether literally by leaving town, or by putting up so many barriers to intimacy that the people who love them feel as if they're stranded on the other side of a wall too high to climb over.

5 The Skeptic has a limited emotional repertoire and is uncomfortable with anyone else's displays of emotion.

Like the housekeeper who doesn't do windows, Skeptics don't "do" feelings. The world of emotions is virtually off-limits for them, because, due to the early trauma they've put in the vacuum cleaner bag of their unconscious (and never reviewed), most of their feelings have been shut down.

While they may be able to get out some anger, they generally minimize their feelings with a joke. They're not usually in touch with their sorrow, grief, or fear, and they're certainly not in touch with their joy. Emotions are too precarious for them. Getting into their feelings would take them into the place of remembering what once happened, the thing that made them Skeptics in the first place, and so, rather than venturing into the jungly outback of their emotions, they'll make another witty joke and carry on.

Skeptics are like an extreme form of the Cool Cucumber. It's not enough that they keep their own emotions to a whisper; they don't want you emoting all over them either. If you do, they'd have to admit that the world of emotions exists—for some people anyway. So they try to jolly you out of your feelings, by cynicism, by minimizing what's going on, by trying to distract you, or, if all else fails, by just leaving.

6 They have worlds you can't get into, and they retreat to them any time you try to get closer to them.

Like guys that hang out with their tools and paint cans in the garage, Skeptics are basically loners. The private little worlds they've created, whether a three-room walk-up apartment, a 17,000-acre ranch, or a special spot in nature, are *theirs,* and they really don't want you to be there with them. That's because these hideaways and urban shelters are really cocoons for their broken spirits, the only place on earth where they can really feel safe. If you invade their sanctuary, it feels to them as if they no longer have anywhere that's safe. You want to bring your love to bear on their painful isolation, but they can't take it. To them, love equals pain. So they're always trying to retreat to their private places because, unlike human beings, places can't hurt them.

7 A few Skeptics do manage to overcome their fear of love and are amazed and overjoyed when they discover what love has to offer.

Since Skeptics come from the farthest extreme of doubt and negativity about love, those few who actually do find it are usually astonished and deeply grateful. That's because, for them, what truly seemed impossible has actually come to pass.

Not many Skeptics find real love. By real love, I mean a relationship in which they are consciously and growthfully participating. (Most Skeptics, if they make it into a relationship, are just hanging out there, while their partners are trying to wake them up, make them over, or significantly change them.) But when a Skeptic does find love, and chooses to do the work of loving, he or she feels great joy.

This love often comes as the result of life-changing crisis that shocks them to their senses, intensive therapy to deal with their original wound, or a partner who genuinely loves them and enjoys some other qualities about them beside their characteristic cynicism. For even a Skeptic, this can make the terror of loving a risk worth taking.

Why We Love Skeptics

Believe it or not, Skeptics are fun. Their nonstop witticisms, self-deprecations, and cynical worldviews are usually expressed in a very captivating way. Since the rest of us don't believe the world is as bad as the Skeptics keep telling us, we really can't believe that they actually see it that way. As a consequence, instead of being taken down by their jocular negativity, we're often happy to go along for the ride. When they say, in effect, "Eat, drink, and be merry for tomorrow we die," and laugh their heads off about it, we laugh with them because we have no idea that in the dark part of their hearts, they really do hold such a disparaging view of life.

Their caustic comments about politics, pollution, the economy, or their own future always have more than a grain of truth in them, and so we can't help but be amused. Because of its unvarnished truth—Skeptics always call a spade a spade—their black humor can be oddly refreshing.

Other personality types, Fantasizers and People Pleasers in particular, are also attracted to Skeptics because they represent a challenge. These types want to be the ones who finally show the Skeptics what love is, what a wonderful experience a relationship can be. Ever-optimistic, they imagine that with their sunny outlooks and indefatigable efforts, they can bring even the most diehard Skeptics around.

How They Drive Us Crazy

The consistency of their negativity gets wearing, as we discover the depth to which it has a hold on them. It's fun to listen a few caustic jokes about how nothing is, has been, or ever will be all right, but a steady diet of this can erode even the sunniest outlook. Life just isn't that bad.

But where the Skeptics really take a toll is that they're relationship teases. They present themselves as available, but soon it becomes clear that it is up to you to break down their walls of defensiveness. Given this, romance can become a battle in which you try to prove that love is worth having, and they get out their bazookas to prove that you're wrong.

Skeptics aren't comfortable when would-be lovers or suitors get too close, and so they put up whatever barriers they can to keep you from puncturing their worldview. They decide you're not appropriate, they tell you that you won't like them when you find out who they really are, or they just disappear and never call you again.

To protect themselves, Skeptics are emotional and physical Houdinis. They often have a great disappearing act—they'll invite you out on a date and then never show up; they'll woo you for a month and then disconnect their phone; they'll spend a weekend with you and then go off for two weeks to nobody-knows-where; they'll marry you and then, instead of talking to you, spend all their time with their short-wave radio.

They drive you crazy because they pull you in and then push you away. They obviously have deep feelings somewhere—where else could all that cynicism come from?—but they systematically deny your feelings and stonewall your approach. For the person who was somehow lured in and then understandably (but erroneously) expecting to have a a an actual relationship with a Skeptic, it's a shock to suddenly find yourself alone.

What's Really Going On?

Whether or not they're consciously aware of it, *Skeptics have experienced a profound betrayal in love. This is their emotional wound* and as a result, they have a very hard time trusting anyone or anything. Their emotional issue is trust. Since this betrayal was immense, and, in spite of any possible opportunities for healing, has remained unaddressed, for the Skeptic, the world is indeed a place where love has equaled pain.

For example, Larry was three years old when his mother became seriously ill and began the long arduous process of dying of breast cancer. Day after day he sat at the foot of her bed, asking his dad when she would get up and play with him again. His dad kept saying he didn't know, but any day now she'd probably be feeling better and she and Larry could go for a walk in the park.

Then came the day when Larry came home from school and his mother wasn't in the bed at all. When Larry asked where she was, his father said, simply, "Well, I guess she went to the park by herself; we'll have to wait and see if she comes back."

It wasn't until several years later, thinking Larry was now old enough to understand the concept of death, that his father finally told him his mother had died.

Larry had loved his mother very much and early in his childhood had been almost inseparable from her. He felt betrayed by her death, but even more by the fact that during her final days she had never told him that she was dying. It was one thing for her to have left; it was quite another that by keeping silent, she had lied to him. He also felt betrayed by his father, who didn't tell him the truth after her death. His was a double wound—of both loss and betrayal. After that, Larry could trust no one, and the world never seemed to him what it was to other people. His trust in life itself was shattered.

Other breaches of trust involve abandonment. For example, Tom, another Skeptic I know, had a twin brother who committed suicide in high school. Rather than grieving openly, Tom adopted a cynical outlook that masked the horrific pain and sense of betrayal he felt at his brother's abandonment of him. Over time, his sardonic attitude took on a darkly humorous tone, and eventually he made a very successful career for himself as a stand-up comedian. But his emotional life has been less successful, and he now uses prostitutes exclusively, so he won't have to deal with a woman's "emotional involvement" with him.

Peter was five, his brother seven, and his little sister two, when, because of a sudden bankruptcy brought on by his father's gambling, his parents suddenly divorced, leaving his mother in a financial crisis. Wanting to keep her family together but unable to do so, Peter's mother allowed him to be adopted by a family at church who had always taken a fancy to him and were unable to have a child of their own.

This betrayal in Peter's young life was devastating because among his siblings he was singled out for this experience. He was sent off to live with strangers, while his brother and sister remained at home, seemingly part of an intact family. Although his mother and siblings were struggling financially and lived in terrible poverty while Peter lived in luxury and comfort with his adoptive parents, he nevertheless felt totally rejected and betrayed. This sense of betrayal became more vivid by the year, when, because of his mother's embarrassment about the discrepancy between her other children's circumstances and Peter's, she totally withdrew from him without announcing that she was. He never saw his brother and sister again.

Wary of relationships as an adult, Peter expects betrayal, and although he's been married two times, he has been sexually betrayed by both his wives—betrayals which, in both instances, he precipitated.

Other breaches of trust occur when the basic care that each of us can legitimately expect from our parents is somehow withdrawn or withheld. Children unconsciously develop a sense that life itself cannot be trusted when protection isn't given or nourishment is withheld.

Carol was the youngest of six children when an epidemic of childhood diseases swept through the household, causing her mother to become exhausted and unavailable. Rather than being able to feed little Carol, her mother left her waiting alone for hours without being fed while she looked after the other children.

Carol started out whimpering, then began crying, but when hours went by and she didn't get fed, she finally gave up and stopped crying altogether. She would be in a state of starvation when her mother finally did come to feed her. In her unconscious mind Carol internalized this betrayal and gave up on ever getting the nourishment she needed.

As an adult in relationships, she finds that she is always somehow "starving." The person she loves doesn't give her enough time, or she has to wait so long for attention that by the time it finally comes she has already given up and can't receive what is given. She keeps replaying this story of her infancy where she was wordless, and as an adult she doesn't know how to express the needs she secretly hopes will be fulfilled by her spouse or lover. To cover her deep sense of betrayal, she's convinced herself that she's better off alone, because that way she can meet her own needs and doesn't have to rely on anyone else. Of course, as always in the past, she's still starving.

These deep betrayals and breaches of trust are never deeper than when a child is verbally or sexually abused by a parent or another close person. We expect those who occupy the parental roles to be our nurturers and to hold the place of protecting the unfolding of our development. When an uncle or parent steps through that role and becomes a sexual abuser, when a mother gets up every morning violently screaming at her children about how worthless they are, a child feels desperate and abused.

People who have experienced such overwhelming violations in childhood have difficulty trusting in adulthood. Indeed, trust is never a given, but always a slow, painful journey for them.

Such breaches of trust utterly change a child's worldview. Rather than seeing life—and the universe—as holding a whole range of possibilities which include both the bad and the good, to the Skeptic, the good world has vanished. It's as if a curtain has been drawn down, and now only the bad world remains. It's because these betrayals occur so young and then are clouded over by lies or silence that they create such a deep wound.

Having been betrayed by his parents, the child is now walled off alone in a world of emotional anguish to which his *loving* parents have conscripted him. It is precisely because this betrayal occurs in the place of the greatest love—it isn't perpetrated by a schoolmate, teacher, or stranger, but by the one person the child believed he could count on no matter what—that the wound is so ghastly and huge.

When children experience a betrayal of this dimension, they feel as if they were fools to have ever trusted in the first place. That's why they construct a world and a worldview that says the world's no good; you can't count on anybody. It's as if knowing this could protect them from ever getting into such an excruciatingly vulnerable place again. If I always keep this in mind, I'll be safer than if I let my guard down, the Skeptic says (unconsciously) to himself. This is why Skeptics can't trust, and that's why love, if they ever really find it, truly is a miracle.

What Skeptics Have to Teach Us

Skeptics can do a good job of awakening our own skepticism; after all they're authorities on it. It's good to take some things with a grain of salt, to look below the surface, not to be complete Pollyannas. Life does have its disasters, betrayals, and unhappy endings, and it's important for the rest of us, especially People Pleasers and Fantasizers, to factor that into our thinking.

They also teach us that sometimes a challenge isn't worth the taking. Some people really *don't* want to be loved, or won't do the emotional work that they'd have to in order to be able to let you love them. Discretion is the better part of valor. Skeptics remind us to respect our own limits, to remember that most of the time, people are who they tell you they are, and all the good will and the best efforts in the world can't talk them out of it. Instead of trying to convince them to change, perhaps we need to learn the compassion of respecting them just as they are.

What Skeptics Needs to Learn About Relationships

People who have issues with trust are in relationships precisely to learn how to trust. Skeptics need to understand that it is through *gradually* developing trust within your relationships that this healing will occur. You're not alive—or in a relationship—just to keep living behind the wall of your lack of trust. If you do, you'll just keep shoving everyone out of your life and always end up alone. Or, if you're in a relationship, you'll always be creating distance between yourself and the person you love because, in your mind, he or she will never be worthy of trust.

What Skeptics Can Do to Come Into Balance

1 Identify your betrayal issues and deal with them.

Skeptics have adapted to the betrayals of early childhood with compensating behavior that seems to give them a sense of control of their world. Many times these betrayal issues were so buried in childhood that they remain unconscious. For your own healing, and with the promised payoff of a better relationship, bring these betrayal issues up to consciousness, confront them, and then take action to resolve them.

In most instances this will require counseling or therapy. Going through the stages of identifying the single event or ongoing experience of betrayal—feeling your anger about it, touching in to your sorrow, feeling compassion for yourself, moving into the forgiveness that will allow you to let go of some of your skepticism and start trusting little by little—all these are necessary steps to your healing.

2 If you do have a relationship, stay conscious.

Since if you're in a relationship your first inclination will be to prove that it won't work, or that, like every other relationship, it too will come to a bad end, start checking your emotional reactions. Each time there's even the tiniest betrayal you'll need to identify it, express your anger, and ask for what you need to resolve it.

For example, your husband flirted with an attractive woman at the party; you find it unforgivable; you need him to apologize, ask you for forgiveness, and promise to be more respectful of you the next time you're out together. Having done this, you will be able to continue the relationship because you took an emotional step. Resolution will come when he can ask for, and you can give, forgiveness. Instead of being stuck in betrayal and a lack of trust, you can move on.

Or, if the betrayal is too great, resolution may require that you consciously decide to end the relationship. For example if your husband has had a series of affairs which are to you, in spite of his apologies, unforgivable because of the magnitude of the breach of trust, rebuilding a trustful view of life may necessitate that you move on.

3 Give love a chance.

To overcome your inability to trust, which leads to greater and greater isolation and loneliness, you need to stretch your boundaries by accepting that a relationship is itself the healing experience for the betrayal you experienced as a child. Learning to trust is a process. It's a process for all of us, even when there hasn't been a big betrayal. But when there has been a big betrayal, there are a great many steps to learning to trust again—or perhaps for the first time. Love doubters need to open their hearts and try to trust just a little bit more.

You will be able to do this when you allow yourself to take note of the fact that along with experiences of violation and betrayal, you have also been given many experiences of love. The more you allow yourself to acknowledge the love you've been given, the more you take in the love of all the people—friends, children, grandmothers, grandfathers, total strangers, and random appreciators of you—who have been sent to share your life with you, the more your issues of trust will gradually subside.

To see how loved you actually are, each day write down the things that have occurred that make you feel loved. There are a great many experiences of the goodness of life and of our own well-being that are simple gifts of the universe—a sunny day, the fact that you do have a place to come home to, a smile from a stranger, someone who shows up to help you when you are in trouble. As you begin, you may see that many of experiences in which you can feel "loved" aren't very personal or intimate. Don't discount them, though. This is a beginning. As you take note of them, you'll have to start undermining your skepticism. See, life isn't all black and hopeless and untrustworthy. The more you take note of your experiences of love (and anchor them in your mind by writing them down) the more you will feel loved.

4 Do something for others.

One of the things that keeps Skeptics in their skepticism is that they're alone with it—practically all of the time. The way to get out of our misery is, quite literally, to get out of it.

When you are giving to others, your own misery, no matter how devastating, takes a back seat.

One woman I know was continually molested by her father and the two uncles her father had moved into the second house on their farm. She said she trusted no one and lived in a rage at God until years later, when a teenage girl who had been repeatedly molested herself told this woman she looked so kind that the young girl knew she could trust the woman to listen to her story.

Broken open by this teenager's story and her innocent trust, this woman realized that other people beside herself were suffering. She turned her anguish into service, and now she runs a home for sexually abused young women.

No matter what your wound, you can transform it.

A Meditation for Skeptics

I'm ready to pull down my walls now. I was deeply wounded and I have great compassion for myself. But I'm willing to give up my cynicism and receive some goodness from the world. I'm even willing to work to receive this goodness. I'm ready to venture into love.

Balancing Affirmations

This is a new day.

Nothing's so bad you can't get over it. Nothing.

When I offer my wound as a gift of healing, it will be transformed and I will be transformed.

Love is the only thing that can save me.

I want to choose love.

5

THE WORKAHOLIC

**"I don't know if I'm free. I'll have to check
my schedule."**

WORKAHOLICS ARE THE ACTIVITY ORGANIZERS AND
schedule jugglers of the relationship types. You would never
say, "Get a life!" to a Workaholic. A Workaholic has a life—
or two or three of them; enough to share with you and still
have a few left over for himself.

The Workaholic is busy with a capital B. She has four
projects due in two weeks—and is volunteering as her son's
soccer coach; he is running a law practice, building a house,
and driving 300 miles every other weekend to visit his kids.
Workaholics are great at getting lots done, but somehow
they always have more to do.

They tend to exist on little sleep, and contribute a great
deal to the bottom line of whatever business they put their

minds to, because they give 110 percent. They work not for attention, glory, or praise, like Attention Seekers do, but for the pure satisfaction of a job well done. They are the CEOs, self-made businesspeople, and entrepreneurs among us. They are competent and complex—whether they're running a gardening business or a major corporation, they can keep their finger on the pulse of a multitude of items and issues at once. Generally more competent, skillful, and knowledgeable than artistic, their creativity shows up in the way they shuffle and parlay their commitments to achieve their own ends.

Tom, married seven years, is a high-powered political consultant who works late most every evening and also on the weekends. His job is "important." He takes at least one vacation without his wife every year because he is so exhausted. It's a "guy thing," he says; he needs time to wander around and unwind alone. At home he has a second office in a separate building—the converted garage of their house—in which he spends every weekend while Ellen amuses herself at the gym or by going out with her girlfriends.

When he does manage to get home at a decent hour after a long hard day at the office, he'll take her out to dinner. They always have a nice time. But the truth is, Tom really doesn't want a relationship. In fact, he's often been accused by Ellen of just wanting her as a showpiece for public occasions. She's right, he does enjoy taking her with him when he needs a trophy wife on his arm, but he also says he really loves her. When they're at home alone though, he always gets up early and leaves for the gym before she wakes up. If he should happen to encounter her in the morning over coffee and toast, he locks himself in the bathroom and takes a long shower until he's ready to head for the car, because "It's too early to talk about anything serious."

Once a year Tom and Ellen take a vacation together. They always go somewhere that Ellen chooses, hoping that away from work, they'll have time for an emotional connection. Usually, it doesn't happen. Instead, while Tom plays golf and tennis, Ellen gets massages and goes shopping. They both relax and unwind and have fancy dinners together each evening, but Ellen isn't allowed to bring up anything too "intense" to "ruin" their good time they're having. At the end, they always have photographs taken to show what a wonderful time they had on vacation. Then they go back home and back to their routine, where Ellen longs for more togetherness, while Tom, in between projects, tells her to stop complaining.

Telltale Signs of a Workaholic

- You're always busy.

- You're highly successful and overcommitted.

- You put people off with delays and continually emerging "other" priorities.

- You prefer to share activities rather than conversation.

- You are admired for being able to do so many things at once.

A Closer Look: Distinguishing Characteristics of Workaholics

1 The Workaholic always has a project or an activity already scheduled that conflicts with whatever you want to do with him or her.

Workaholics genuinely believe that they want a relationship but somehow have always arranged their lives in such a way that they really don't have time for it. Everything they're doing is important—and they're not just a-whistling Dixie. The things they cite as conflicting with whatever you want to do with them are, by anybody's standards, worthwhile, important, and certainly need to be done. For example, that visit from his parents whom he hasn't seen for eight years certainly can't be chalked off his schedule. Neither can the corporate meeting that's going to take her out of town for a week. Neither can her children, or that discussion with his ex-wife about their daughter's braces. Neither can the overtime he's working to pay off his credit cards.

The Workaholic always has a million excuses, all of them good, for why he or she can't be with you at any particular time. In fact, all the rest of us who are just looking for a simple white lie to miss a single personal engagement could run to a Workaholic and find a whole encyclopedia of them.

2 Workaholics put you off.

"Not this week, maybe next." "Not this Christmas, maybe next." "Not tomorrow, maybe on Thursday." "Let's wait and see what happens. I don't know what I've got scheduled." "Gee I'd love to take a vacation with you but my summer's pretty booked. What about fall?" "Okay, what about fall?" "Well, I don't know what my schedule's going to be then. Let's talk about it once September rolls around."

Whatever you'd like to plan, you can count on them to not get into the planning with you. They keep things vague, open-ended, continually rolling the calendar into the distant, mysterious future, keeping your hopes up and yet when the time comes, never quite finding a way to fulfill them—at least not at the level you'd prefer. You get an hour of their time when you asked for a day, a day instead of a week. "I'm just calling to tell you I'm thinking of you, but I really don't have time to talk right now." "I know we agreed to spend the evening together, but I've got to go meet the electrician over at the construction site." And all the time they're telling you how sorry they are, because they, too, really wanted to take the day, the week, the weekend—if only they weren't so busy.

3 When they are with you, Workaholics are distracted by other commitments.

Workaholics have a slew of excuses for why they can't be with you for the special events or even ongoing activities of a relationship. And when you finally do nail them down to a specific occasion, they will find a million ways of not continuing the conversation, not having the argument that could resolve an old issue, not going deeper emotionally, not working out something specific for the future. You may be out to dinner, but he has his cell-phone with him and takes all the calls from his office. Or she has to call home every five minutes to see how the kids are doing because she's so nervous about leaving them alone.

Workaholics are always running off to this or that thing, which prevents them from being with you in the here and now. While on the macro level they're always busy with the seemingly legitimate concerns of their own life, on the micro level, if you actually try to corner them for a relationship experience, they'll find a whole passel of ways to not quite be there with you. They've got a headache. They're waiting for that call. Whoops, they just remembered, they've got to go pick up that stuff at the cleaners. They can't take your relationship to the next level because they've always got a project.

This is the year she's remodeling her condo. Or, he's decided to build a boat, it's his lifetime dream, and five minutes after you had your first date is exactly the minute he decided he had to get to work on it. It's going to take years of course; building Kon Tiki was a piece of cake compared to what he's decided to undertake. Or else she's writing a book—and you know how fragile the creative process is. Don't call her between nine and noon, that's when she writes; and don't call her in the afternoon either because that's when she's getting her exercise to make up for sitting in front of the computer all morning.

4 Workaholics want to share activities, not feelings.

Once in a while, Workaholics will slip in a nice little trip where they actually do spend a little personal time with you. Most of the time though, they're off on their own, since they thrive on activities that keep them away from intimacy. They're willing to share an activity with you as long as it keeps them from going too deep with their feelings: scuba diving, baseball games. To them, the world is a chessboard of events and undertakings, all of which need to be fitted into their slots, and all of which have—they think you'll agree—unquestionable value. Joining you in this world of distractions keeps them distracted and encourages you to collude with them in building a world that consists of a million distractions.

At the end of an unsuccessful marriage, which she got into at eighteen because of an unwanted pregnancy, Wanda met a gorgeous man in the grocery store who instantly started courting her. She was delighted because her husband of record, as she by now called him, was a definite stick in the mud. He never wanted to go anywhere or do anything.

In fact, his unwillingness to partake of the pleasures and opportunities she saw all around her was the major reason why, after six years, she had decided to divorce him. When Ben showed up, inviting her to go to motorcycle races, the state fair, and a convention his computer company was having in Dallas, Wanda was delighted. Finally some action, she thought. Finally life's going to be interesting.

All these activities did indeed put some spice in Wanda's life, and six months after her divorce, she felt as if she had entered a new, exciting relationship with Ben and was even contemplating marrying him. About that time, his company offered him a job in Japan. It represented a sizable increase in salary, an opportunity for greater responsibility, and, of course, a chance to see another part of the world. He invited Wanda and her daughter to go along with him. Surprised by this turn of events, Wanda nevertheless decided that this was also a once-in-a-lifetime opportunity for her. She packed up her daughter and two months later, Ben, Wanda, and her little girl headed off for Japan.

Once in Japan, however, Ben revealed his true colors. Overwhelmed as he legitimately was by his new responsibilities, he was gone day and night, while Wanda stayed home trying to learn Japanese and taking a class in Ikebana flower arranging. Her daughter, enrolled in a bilingual school, quickly picked up the language and made new friends, but Wanda felt shut out and neglected. She couldn't work, she couldn't speak the language, and apart from her early weeks of fascination with the new and unusual culture, she felt abandoned and lonely.

As long as they were in Japan, Wanda chalked it up to the responsibilities of his new job. But when his six-month tour of duty was completed and they returned home, Wanda saw that the pattern he had established there proved not to be an exception but the rule. Day after day Ben vanished early to the office, enthralled with the new computer knowledge he had acquired in Japan and eager to share it with his colleagues.

Exhausted from these long days at work, he claimed he needed to "do something different" at night and on weekends. Week after week, Ben found things that just happened to take him away from home every weekend. Unless Wanda was willing to join him in one of his activities—shopping for motorcycles, looking at garden tools, joining his buddies' wives while he and his men friends watched innumerable sports events—she wouldn't see Ben. Rather than wanting to get to know her, to build a firm emotional foundation for their relationship, the longer they were in it, the more distracted Ben became.

The very quality that she had at first so enjoyed about Ben, his willingness, indeed his insistence, on continually creating new and unusual experiences, she now recognized as an almost pathological fascination with distractions. The man whose active life had so enthralled her became an absentee partner. After a year and a half, Wanda split up with him, heaving a sigh of relief that she had avoided a second divorce by never marrying him.

While men with their widgets, gadgets, and toys seem to be the masters of distractibility, the Workaholic doesn't only come in male form. Women too can be so preoccupied with work, with cleaning the house, with their children (and what greater excuse than that your children need attention), they too qualify by droves as Workaholics. Like men, they may think and actually believe that they want a relationship, but when it comes right down to it, they don't want to get too involved either.

Katherine, a lesbian and a successful business executive with her own small corporation, fell in love with Charlotte and was delighted to have made this new relationship. However, each time Charlotte proposed romantic weekends or sharing the pleasures of creating a household—remodeling, working in the garden—Katherine always found a reason why she had to be at the office. Not only that, but the only vacations she proposed were the ones where Charlotte could join her at business conferences.

Even at the outset, when she was falling madly in love, Katherine admitted to herself that her primary commitment was to making her business a success. What she liked about Charlotte, she said, was that she was a "low-maintenance lover." In truth, though, she was using Charlotte simply as an available companion, not taking the time to create any emotional depth. Soon their relationship became shallow and uninteresting, and within two years it crashed on the rocks of Katherine's corporate executiveship.

5 Workaholics don't really want a deep connection. They don't want to get too emotionally involved.

Take the dinner conversation too deep and they'll talk about how great the garlic bread is. Get into the realm of your feelings and they'll talk, vaguely of course, about some possible future vacation. Talk about your family or theirs, and they'll distract you from the discussion. Like Cool Cucumbers, they don't want to get into deep emotional waters, but in their case, rather than active emotional suppression, they just keep moving to avoid feeling. They won't tell you directly that they "don't want to deal with such things," they'll just say that they "just want to accomplish something." If they don't have the courage to admit that they want to accomplish something, they'll just keep holding their ten million projects out in front of you like a decoy—as if you and everyone else on the planet agree that accomplishments are the one thing in life worth undertaking.

Workaholics talk a good line. They talk about wanting to have a relationship, but the truth is, they like the idea better than the reality.

Deeply hurt from her previous marriage to the father of her two children, Michelle was at first delighted to meet Jim, who seemed to come along at just the right time. The children, now nine and eleven, were of an age where she felt comfortable starting to date seriously. But almost the moment after Jim arrived, Michelle started sashaying backward and sideways out of his life. Suddenly her children became an urgent priority. "I have to take Mark to Little League practice," she'd say. "I have to take Cathy to Brownies." "I have to stay home with them at night because they're scared to be alone." "I have to be there when their father brings them home on Sunday afternoons so they won't feel stranded or abandoned."

All her excuses were, of course, legitimate. Everyone knows that children need a mother, but her involvement seemed excessive. As she piled one excuse on top of another, Jim became frustrated, fearing that in actuality Michelle didn't want a relationship with him. Still, he tried various strategies: taking her on a vacation, suggesting they go to therapy, encouraging them to take weekends away from the kids at a motel where they could have a romantic experience. Finally he gave up in despair because the more he approached her with creative solutions to "the problem of the children's needs," the more she seemed to withdraw from him.

Whether they're busy saving the planet, running the

country, raising their kids, or are simply unable to get out from behind the newspaper or to stop "surfing the Net," the purpose of all this frantic activity is to keep Workaholics from intimacy. These activities and habits—commitments, really—crowd the spaces that could be reserved for a relationship.

Like the spiritual practitioner who is forever meditating and never comes down from the mountain to taste of real life, Workaholics are always somehow teetering on the brink, camped out on the outskirts of a real relationship. Rather than using their activities as an adjunct to life, these people are distracting themselves from the juice of true intimacy by being forever elsewhere involved.

Why We Love Workaholics

We love Workaholics because they have energy, they bring variety to our lives, they give us a sense that life is interesting and worth living, a smorgasbord of possibilities and activities that are there for the taking.

They give our lives texture and relieve our boredom. They inspire us with their elaborate time-balancing acts; they seem to do the impossible. Often they make our lives easier because of all they do—we benefit from the houses they build, their six-figure salaries, their knowledge of fine wines. Sometimes they even structure our lives. That's because in being so focused on work themselves they're often also very good at seeing what we should be doing and in aiding us in developing our own careers. Helping us on top of everything else that they're doing is also a breeze and a joy, because, of course, it's more work, and so, of course, they're up for it. Those of us who have trouble figuring out what do are particularly drawn to the frantically focused world of the Workaholic because it's alive with goals and purpose.

We love Workaholics, too, because they're so strong-willed, clear, and decisive. They're wonderful providers and are often powerful and interesting human beings.

How They Drive Us Crazy

Workaholics put you off. They're always putting you off. Potential lovers, spouses, and close friends are turned off by them because, one way or another, Workaholics keep intimacy at bay.

We get tired of waiting for them to come home, to call, to have a free weekend. Because they're always busy, they make you feel rejected, as if their motorcycle, newspaper, the Dow Jones average, the new business plan, or the latest research on the best spas of their world is more important to them than you are. At their worst, they can make you feel uninteresting and valueless. Eventually you feel unwanted and in the way.

Workaholics are also good at inducing guilt when partners complain about their lack of attention. Don't you want to stop global warming? Don't you want the big car that he's working so hard to pay for? Don't you care about how the children turn out? If you protest or try to explain, they'll probably argue with you. And, of course, they'll always be right—at least in their own minds—so how can you argue with them? Just look at all the important things they're doing.

What's Really Going On?

At the psychological level, *the Workaholic's emotional wound is abandonment.* Whether it is obvious, such as the loss of a parent in early life, or more subtle, such as a sense of emotional abandonment engendered, in many cases, by one or more Workaholic parents—at the root of the Workaholic's behavior are the profound feelings of sorrow surrounding their abandonment, which have never been acknowledged or felt. In childhood, they didn't have the emotional wherewithal to deal with their abandonment, and so they are stuck in unresolved grief.

In adulthood, rather than going through the emotional process of grieving moving through the anger, sorrow, for giveness, and acceptance, which could finally lead to resolution—Workaholics put off venturing into these deep emotional waters. It's as if early on they figured out that you can't feel and keep moving at the same time, and so they learned to keep moving so they wouldn't have to feel. The longer they live, the more stuffed-down feelings they have to deal with, and the more they need to desperately keep moving to avoid feeling. They end up reproducing in adulthood the abandonment they once felt as a child, either by abandoning their own emotions through overwork, or by abandoning those who love them by being too busy and distracted.

Not all Workaholics experienced abandonment from Workaholic parents. Some come from families in which there were too many children for there to be focused attention on any individual child. Or perhaps a disabled child required a great deal of attention while the rest of the kids were left to fend for themselves. Others experienced the obvious abandonment—an absentee father, a mother who ran off—that leaves a deep scar and an unfelt sorrow.

But it isn't only physical abandonment that creates these feelings of loss. Sometimes, because their parents were neglectful, or, in an odd turnaround, because their parents were so overinvolved or overprotective, these children feel *emotionally* abandoned. In one way or another their parents didn't bring them the kind of nurturing attention they needed, so they feel as if they have no safe haven emotionally.

For example, Dick's mother was so emotionally out to lunch that she never made meals for him, never taught him even the basics of personal hygiene, and when he was a young man, never talked to him about brushing his teeth or washing his hair. As a teenager he felt alienated and was continually ridiculed at school for his bad breath, greasy hair, and rumpled clothes.

Jack, on the other hand, was raised by a suffocating and overinvolved mother *and* grandmother. His father was always away at—you guessed it—work. His mother and Nana would never let him go out of the house without a muffler, a sweater, his shoes tied, and a handkerchief. Nor would they let him go out after dark. Nor would they let him go to the homes of his friends. This constituted *emotional* abandonment because his mother and grandmother abandoned their appropriate role of nurturing the development of his independence. He couldn't turn to them for help in developing his own personality. All they did was suffocate him.

Pretty soon, Jack was sneaking around, finding legitimate excuses to get out of the house—school, work, sports, a series of jobs. At seventeen he left home. Speaking of his childhood, he said he feels as if he had *no* parents—his father was never around; his mother and grandmother "fed off" him. The only thing he got comfort from was keeping busy. Apart from all his activities, there was no emotional connection for him.

No matter how the abandonment occurred, it is exceedingly painful to the soon-to-be-adult Workaholic, for children who are abandoned gradually come to feel unloved and unworthy of attention. At first this feeling may register sharply as a painful emotional rejection, but being continually subjected to the distractions or outright disappearance of their parents, these children combat their emotional pain by developing distractions of their own: "Hey Mom, I joined the Little League. I've got practice. I won't be home for supper." Or, "I'm going out with my friends," says the teenager, disappearing every night. One way or another they make sure that their lives, too, are so overscheduled and full of distractions that they don't notice the pain of the missed emotional connection.

Sometimes Workaholics-in-the-making create superficial distractions precisely in order not to feel their grief. One Workaholic told me that, as a child, she kept repeatedly messing up her room so that she could be endlessly cleaning it up, thereby avoiding feeling her pain about her father's alcoholism. Another reported going out to the marshes near his house and building fort after fort in order not to feel his pain about his mother's emotional coldness. Still another said he was always out applying for jobs under the guise of trying to save enough money to go someplace special, because he was so hurt by his father's absence in Vietnam. One way or another these busy children grow up to be distracted adults, in time abandoning others as they themselves were once abandoned.

As this pattern deepens, the Workaholic's only sense of value lies in his accomplishment or activity. The busier they are, the more fulfilled they imagine they will be. By never going to a deeper level and seeing if, in fact, they do feel fulfilled, they keep their lives so full of activities that busyness and exhaustion pass for satisfaction.

A hidden burden of Workaholics is the unconscious feeling that all their achievements are really who they are. Since the Workaholic has never faced his real feelings of loss and longing for intimacy, sometimes, through the haze of exhaustion, they must face the frightening questions: "Do I have value apart from all the work I've done, the collection of goodies I've amassed, the activities I'm continually engaged in?" "Who would I be if I stopped working?" The Workaholic is always *doing* instead of *being*, acting instead of feeling, to try to escape the pain of the ever-elusive emotional connection.

Workaholics are in pain about their loss. The pain set in on them long before they could figure it out and they developed a pattern of adaptation that has served them as well as it could. Going into the arena of emotional connection was too painful, because no matter how much they tried to connect, it didn't work. Either the situation was totally hopeless to begin with—their parents had already died and left them, or it got progressively worse—their parents were too distracted to give the appropriate emotional nurturance. No matter what these children did, one way or another they felt abandoned. Disappointed at the outset by the limited emotional possibilities of their early relationships, these Workaholics-in-the-making learned to distract themselves to avoid feeling the deep grief they experienced over their abandonment.

This pattern, to a smaller degree, is obvious when a Workaholic's relationship ends. Rather than being willing to go through the pain of healing so they can love again, Workaholics often feel so overwhelmed that they don't go through all the steps that could lead to emotional resolution. Instead they try to distract themselves with work or the next relationship so they won't be caught off-guard by their feelings once again.

The Difference Between a Workaholic and Everyone Else

As we all know, to be human is to be busy from time to time, to be beset by circumstances that require inordinate attention. An illness, a family crisis, a particularly demanding project at work can distract anyone's attention for a significant period of time. But the difference between a Workaholic and everyone else is that the Workaholic has distractions as a *modus operandi*, the way things always are with them, whereas a regular person has distractions as a counterpoint to the more smooth sailing flow of life.

In today's frantic, high-pressured world, workaholism is the norm, and those of us who move at a slower pace, who refuse to work overtime or schedule twenty-five social commitments in the next two weeks, are looked at askance. The difference is that true Workaholics not only choose but celebrate this as a lifestyle. They use work almost exclusively as their source of fulfillment, while the rest of us race around against our will, struggling to make time for the intimacy we crave.

Workaholics would probably deny that they are trying to avoid emotional intimacy. They'd say that every single thing they are doing is necessary, essential to the forward movement of their life, and that, in fact, if they weren't doing it, they wouldn't be able to have a relationship at all. "Do you think I like going to work?" they'll say sometimes, distracting you from the real issue. "Do you think I really love going to all these meetings?" "But I *have* to take care of the kids," they insist. "I can't just go off and leave them!" The telltale clue is that a Workaholic is always distractedly busy while the rest of us are only distracted from time to time.

What Workaholics Have to Teach Us

Workaholics remind us that the world is full of things to do, pleasures to explore, responsibilities to undertake, information to be digested. As they continually show us the complexity of life through their multitude of personal, professional, and recreational undertakings, they keep us tuned in to the rich variety of life.

Workaholics also show us that we *can* divide our attention, manage a number of different activities and undertakings, and focus on more than one thing at once. In a world where you have to answer the phone, the fax, the Jehovah's Witness at the door; recycle your bottles, cans, newspapers, plastic bottles, and bags; go to the laundry, the cleaners, the grocery store, the 7–11, the gym, and church on Sunday, it isn't bad at all to learn how to do ten things at once and move from one thing to another faster than a speeding bullet.

Unlike the Perfectionist, who will never truly get finished (or who will never begin in the first place), Workaholics know that accomplishment has value. They remind us, particularly the Emoters and Fantasizers among us, that sometimes it's important to put aside how we feel about things and just take action.

What Workaholics Need to Learn About Relationships

Workaholics need to know that relationships are the greatest source of our emotional healing. The deep wounds that have prevented you from expressing and exploring your emotions for your whole life are exactly what can be healed when you take the risk of exploring your emotions *in relationship*. Since Workaholics are above all emotion-avoiders, they need to know that one of the greatest gifts of relationship is emotional growth and healing.

What Workaholics have an opportunity to discover is that the experience of emotional connection is one of the greatest activities and most enjoyable experiences we can have in life. As you gradually move through your fears of emotional intimacy, you will discover the emergence of an inner quiet and calm. You will also discover that an emotional connection is not only just as satisfying, but even more satisfying than the flurry of distractions with which you usually keep yourself busy.

We live in a culture where we say we're looking for more peace and quiet, more leisure and relaxation—and, above all, for more intimacy and meaning. Yet the scared part of ourselves—the Workaholic in all of us—is always stirring the kettle and keeping the waters frothy—especially in our relationships. The more you can trust yourself to go into your emotional life, the more sweet and deep your relationships will become.

What Workaholics Can Do to Come Into Balance

Since Workaholics are trying to avoid being emotionally hurt once again, whether or not they've acknowledged how emotionally hurt they once were, their healing comes in the form of experiences that will allow them to tiptoe back into the emotional realm.

1 Give yourself a day off.

Workaholics need to see their busyness as an addiction. They need to address it through an ongoing effort to move away from it and toward another way of experiencing life. So, give yourself a day off. In other words, take a day in which you don't schedule any activities. At first this will seem weird and most likely also uncomfortable. If a day is too long, try half a day. Try an hour. And within the segment of time that you've set aside, do something different. Have a conversation in which, instead of planning an activity, you talk about your feelings. For example, talk about how it feels to not be doing anything. "Do you still like me now that we're not skiing?" "Are you happy just lying here in bed and drinking coffee and looking out at the sunlight?" "What are your dreams for the rest of your life?" Or, "I feel nervous. This is weird. I want to get up and read the paper."

If you're a true Workaholic, you'll notice that not "doing anything" creates feelings of extreme tension. Just as with any other addiction, withdrawal from workaholism will put you in a state so unfamiliar that you will feel extremely uncomfortable. Recognize that this discomfort is natural, and try to go with it. Keep telling yourself that there will be some benefits. Some of them will be scary.

For example, years ago I quit smoking, a habit I had enjoyed and then not-enjoyed for many years. One of the most remarkable discoveries I made after I quit was that it seemed like time almost doubled. Every day I would look at the clock and expect the day to be almost over, only to find that there were several more hours than I expected. At first this was extremely uncomfortable. What would I do now? How would I get through the evening? Gradually I found that I had more time to read, to walk, to have lovely leisurely conversations with friends. Smoking had been a major distraction. Taking it out of my schedule "stretched" time; suddenly it opened and flowed. And in this expanded time, deeper, richer, more spirit-involving experiences took the place of smoking. By giving up my distraction, I had created room for greater depth and beauty in my life.

2 Take some dramatic steps.

Cancel the newspaper, cancel magazine subscriptions, cancel call waiting, cancel all those catalogs full of goodies that you distract yourself by looking at.

In order to figure out what to cancel, go through a day by making a list of how you keep yourself busy. Is it with the phone? With the mail? Other people? With an excessive array of commitments, thumbing through your appointment book that is so overjammed that it's nearly illegible? What would you do if you changed your appointment book from a 5 x 8 to a 2 x 3 inch format? Could you fit your life into it? What would you do with the space you create?

3 Go inward.

The Workaholic needs to move from the outer to the inner world and discover that it's as rich *in here* as it is *out there*. You need to see your emotional life as an activity in itself, the changing nuances of feeling as they shift in a given day from delight to panic to quiet enjoyment, to calm, to fear, to anger, as being of infinite value in themselves.

Since it's the world of emotions that's so scary to the Workaholic, any baby-steps into the emotional world represent movement toward a healing change. For example, the next time you're out with your partner or potential lover, do this exercise. Reveal three random things about yourself, and once you have, encourage the person you're with to reveal three things about him- or herself. These can be trivial things such as, "I'm allergic to shrimp." Or they may be very deep, such as, "My brother is gay and when my parents found out they disowned him. Even now they don't know that he's dying—or that I'm taking care of him in the AIDS hospice." Whatever you choose to reveal, your disclosure will represent some movement into the emotional arena.

After you've made your revelations, ask the person you're with to respond briefly to each of them: "Wow, that's heavy." Or, "It's interesting to know that. So, have you ever had a reaction to shrimp since your first allergic reaction?" Notice how it feels to be responded to in this way. Do you like it? Is it scary? Would you be willing to go a little deeper? If you feel you would, give it a try.

Emotional revelations deepen our encounters with one another. After you've received a response to yours, tiptoe into responding to the other person's revelations to you. See how your feeling of connection deepens; this is what relationships are all about.

4 Share a different kind of experience.

Since Workaholics are activity-aholics, anything other than business-as-usual is frightening to them. The minute you do something different together, you will move into a different part of your psyche. For example, instead of going to play miniature golf, meditate together; instead of making love because you're horny, decide to go to the movies and sit quietly together. Instead of turning on the TV, leave it off and go for a walk around the block. Try standing still instead of moving. Try talking instead of turning on the TV. Try silence instead of action. The more you vary your repertoire, the more you'll have a different experience of yourself and the person you love.

5 Cry. Grieve. Feel your sorrow.

Since the Workaholic has experienced some kind of abandonment—either actual or emotional—this is a great loss. The healing for loss is *grief*. We don't just "get over" these losses, and time does not heal all wounds. Feeling the pain of them does. The feeling of the pain is the grieving process by which we are gradually renewed.

If you're a Workaholic, you need to connect with your tears. Whatever it takes to do that, do it. Whether it's going to the mountains, sitting on a big rock, and letting the tears gradually fall, being in a therapy group where everybody prods you until you break open, or taking the risk of speaking your sorrow to the person you love until, gradually, in that safety you can cry, let the tears begin.

Ian, finally connecting with his pain about his mother's coldness, said that his heart felt like a little wrinkled-up balloon inside his chest. He realized that he had felt a vague sense of sadness, kind of like being on the brink of tears, throughout his childhood, but it wasn't until he fell in love with Carolyn and one night found himself weeping in her arms after making love that he realized how great his pain really was.

There will never be enough distractions to make your pain go away, but grieving about it, truly feeling your sorrow, will bring you to a new day.

A Meditation for Workaholics

I was deeply hurt as a child. Deep down I felt abandoned. That really hurt my spirit. Now I just want to be loved. I'm slowing down to make some room for love to come in.

Balancing Affirmations

There's more to life than all this stuff I'm doing.

Love, too, is a project. And it's more important than anything else I can think of to do.

Love is the greatest achievement.

It's okay to cry.

6

THE PERFECTIONIST

"If you can't do it right, don't do it at all."

THE PERFECTIONIST IS THE MARTHA STEWART–TYPE
person who relishes ordering things—whether it is the napkin drawer, the screws in the garage, or the love lives of all
her friends. If you want a job done well, call in a
Perfectionist. They're experts at knowing how to make
schedules, organize files, and tell other people how to organize or improve themselves.

Perfectionists have incredibly high standards. In fact,
they're always working off an invisible ideal—the perfect
house, the perfect job, the perfect lover. At their best,
Perfectionists also work hard at improving themselves—intellectually, emotionally, financially, spiritually. Perfectionists are
the A students, the impeccable homemakers, the employees
who do their jobs with precision. They make great workers

where organization and attention to detail is required, although they tend to get frustrated at their inability to control every jot and tittle, have trouble delegating, and are devastated when a mistake occurs on their watch.

There's no rest for the Perfectionist. No matter what their situation, one way or another, they're always wanting things to be just a little bit better. If they're in a relationship, they always want it to be a little different—more or less serious—or they want it to be conducted in just a certain way. Whether it's about timing, the way the house is kept, the children are raised, or the furniture is arranged, the Perfectionist always has an idea about exactly how it should be done, as well as a vision of the perfect outcome. If they're not in a relationship, their perfectionism can take the form of having a million ever-changing standards which no potential lover can ever quite fulfill. Since, one way or another Perfectionists are always reaching for an invisible ideal, they can never quite make their peace with what actually exists. They can never just relax into whatever is going on.

Sally was married right out of college to a nice, easygoing guy who worked hard. Together they bought and remodeled a comfortable house in a pleasant neighborhood. However, she was always frustrated with him because he wasn't quite perfect—he worked a little too much, he wouldn't talk about their relationship enough, he had a lot of old sports gear he kept stacked in the front hall closet. So, after eight years, she left him in pursuit of Mr. Perfect, whom, not long after, she thought she had found.

After a few months, however, she realized that he too had flaws—he was depressed and drank too much. Challenged but undeterred, Sally was convinced that she could change him, and took on his difficulties as a project, marshaling a plan for AA, a new job, and antidepressant medication. With the same competence and zeal with which she had created her highly successful secretarial service, she tried to change him. But he was resistant to her self-improvement scheme, and so, after six months of not succeeding (totally unacceptable to a Perfectionist), she left him too.

Three years later, she's still alone, refusing to date because "Nobody's perfect."

Telltale Signs of the Perfectionist

- You believe that things should be perfect.

- You do what you do impeccably.

- You may have trouble committing to a relationship.

- You're "hard on yourself"—and others.

- You have very high standards—for everything.

- Once you're in a relationship, you're always "working on it."

- You tend to be depressed.

A Closer Look: Distinguishing Characteristics of the Perfectionist

1 Perfectionists are hard on themselves.

Perfectionists have very high standards to which they hold themselves. No matter what they're doing—working, cooking, playing—they need to do it "perfectly." If the soufflé falls, if their friend doesn't just love the gift, or they strike out at bat, they consider themselves to have failed totally. As a consequence, they can only do what they're the best at, and they miss exploring all the areas of life in which they are less than perfect. Therefore they are often highly overdeveloped in certain areas but their range of abilities may be limited. It's also hard to get them to try something new, because they can't stand to go through the learning-curve stage where, inevitably, we all make a lot of mistakes.

Perfectionists often choose particular areas to be perfectionistic about: some need what they *do* to be perfect, but can live in sloppy surroundings; others focus their perfectionism on their homes, spouses, or children. Others are all-around picky, needing everything they do—their work, their relationships, and their children—to be perfect, as well as their houses, wardrobes, toolboxes, and cars.

Whatever their particular perfectionistic standards, at bottom Perfectionists can't relax and come to rest. They feel they need to be ever-vigilant, to be sure that life—their house, their job, their relationship—isn't spinning out of control. As a result, the Perfectionist is always in a slight state of anxiety because, of course, in actuality, life cannot be controlled.

2 Nobody ever quite meets their exacting standards.

No matter who they end up choosing, no one is ever quite right for them. A young man I know, age thirty-six and never married, had tried every major method of finding a girl to "settle down with," much of this with his mother's encouragement. He tried dating his father's secretary, going to a video dating service, going on blind dates, having his sister's husband set him up with a nice girl he knew, putting in personals ads, joining the Sierra Club, going to bars, and doing everything that every dating manual on Earth said was a good way to meet the girl of his dreams.

He met hundreds of girls, each time causing an excited flutter in his mother's heart, but every time he found something wrong with them. No matter what positive qualities they brought to a potential relationship, all he could say was, "I can't stand her blue nail polish." "I can't go out with anybody who smokes." "She doesn't want to have children." "She wants to have children right now." "She's too old for me." "She's too young." "She's too short." "She's too tall." "She's got a weird nose." "She leaves towels on the bathroom floor."

Like this young man, Perfectionists can always find enough fault with anybody so that, whoever they are, they're just not quite right. Like Professor Higgins saying, "Why can't a woman be more like a man?" the Perfectionist is saying, "Why can't a woman—and everybody else—be more like my perfectionistic ideal?"

3 Perfectionists are interested in perfecting people.

When a Perfectionist chooses a mate, one way or another, the mate will be a project for him, since the potential perfectibility—or at least improvement—of the other person is what attracts the Perfectionist in the first place. A friend of mine has been married twice. She was attracted to her first husband, she says, "because he was intelligent and kind." Many other people found him arrogant, but she could see his sweet side underneath and "just knew she could help him bring it out." After fourteen years of fighting, in which she tried and tried to get him to be softer, kinder, and more gentle, he got fed up with her and ran off with another woman. Now she's married to a man whose potential as an artist has never quite been quite reached. Once again, she's sure she can help him "become who he's supposed to be."

Another man I know married a woman whose pretty face and bubbly personality lifted his frequently pessimistic spirits. She was grossly overweight, but he "could see the statuesque goddess inside her just waiting to come out." It didn't, of course—in spite of his endless schemes and diet plans. Eventually tired of being embarrassed each time he was out in public with her and realizing his efforts were hopeless, he finally left her.

Like this man, most Perfectionists like the *project* of perfecting the people they love even more than the people themselves, and the one or two traits that attract them are not, in fact, the most powerful draw in their relationship connections.

4 Perfectionists are always disappointed in relationships. Whomever they love "betrays" them.

Since their lover or mate has to be so perfect, sooner or later the person they love will disappoint or betray them. That's because life is imperfect and so are all of us in it, and so, at some point, all the imperfect people the Perfectionist loves will create a situation in which the unacceptable—i.e., totally normal—thing will occur.

One lovely Perfectionist, a young woman I know, told the story of how she just "had to" end her relationship because her boyfriend lost her beach basket. She'd had it for several years, and one day when she and he were driving in the car together they had a terrible mishap. The car hit a bumpy patch on the road and one of its tires fell off. While they were waiting for help to come, she took her basket out of the car and left it at the side of the road. Eventually a stranger arrived and helped them back home. Several hours later, when they were having dinner and she realized that her basket was gone, she blew up at her boyfriend. "How could you do this to me?" she said. "Now that I see how careless you are, I see we can't possibly get married."

The fact that the circumstances were complicated and it had been she herself who'd left the basket by the side of the road completely escaped her. Somehow her lover was responsible. He was supposed to make it perfect no matter how complex the situation actually was.

Along similar lines, when Bob was going on a trip he asked his girlfriend, Maggie, to make the rather complicated reservations for their three-stop trip from Los Angeles to Singapore. Bob changed his mind so many times, insisting that Maggie call the airlines every time he did to make the necessary changes, that by the time they finally arrived on the first leg of the journey, their tickets had been changed in a way that didn't reflect Bob's up-to-the-minute preference.

"How could you do this?" he blew up at her. "I told you a thousand times that I wanted to go from Los Angeles to Honolulu to Singapore."

"That's right," she said. "You told me a thousand times. I can't keep up with you!"

"Well, why don't you just know?" Bob harangued back.

"I don't," Maggie said, "I can't read your mind!" No matter that his "Well, why don't you just know?" question was the height of wild Perfectionistic expectations, Bob, a total Perfectionist, did expect Maggie to perfectly satisfy his every whim. That's why he felt entitled to be enraged.

5 Perfectionists tend to be depressed.

Since Perfectionists are operating from the principle that perfection *can be attained,* they're always disappointed by reality. The glass is always half-empty instead of half-full. "If it isn't one thing it's another!" they say with chagrin and disgust, as if by now all these little—or big—imperfections should have been erased. Such a remark is the consequence of measuring life against the actually unattainable standards of perfection that diehard Perfectionists believe, if not consciously then unconsciously, can actually be attained.

Because their standards are so high, life can never please them; neither can the people they love. Instead of enjoying what they do have (the half-full glass or life as it actually is), they live in a constant state of semi-depression because life is never what, according to their high standards, it should be. In addition, the normal difficulties and disappointments of life (to say nothing of the occasional knotty threads and nasty snarls) all seem like a personal affront to them: "How could the tire blow up on me?" "How could that mistake have slipped by me?" "How could she do this to me?" "How could he be twenty minutes late for our date?" "How could she tell me she didn't like my tie?"

Perfectionists aren't just unhappy in the moment. There seems to be a sort of low-grade pale, gray cloud of depression that follows them around as they move through the normal, variegated, and definitely imperfect vicissitudes of life. Life isn't perfect and they can't make it so. And so they're always a little depressed. They have a hard time enjoying life-as-it-is because they're unable to trust that this is as good as life gets and that as-good-as-it-gets is good enough.

Why We Love Perfectionists

We're drawn to Perfectionists precisely because they do seek perfection. They inspire us. We're amazed by their patience and strength, their will and determination, and their ability to pursue a goal to its perfect end. Through their commitment, their willingness to spend twice as much time and four times as much effort as an ordinary mortal to get their files in perfect order, to paint the bathroom without spilling a drop of paint on the floor, to know the location of every single one of their possessions, to have the relationship conversation until the perfect solution is found, or to imagine the perfect vacation, they remind us to strive to be the best we can be. As a consequence, they elevate our standards of taste and behavior.

We love them because they remind us that somewhere out there, there is an invisible ideal, an example greater and more beautiful than any we've seen. We may not see it at the moment, but in acknowledging its existence, even in invisible realms, perfectionists can open up our awareness to the spiritual realm, where perfection does, in fact, exist.

How They Drive Us Crazy

Potential lovers are turned off and mates and spouses are frustrated because, with their constant harping and setting of standards, nothing you do can make a Perfectionist happy. As one Perfectionist said when starting out in a new relationship, "Right now you may love all these little things I'm explaining about how to set the table or store the paint cans, but after awhile it'll drive you crazy." He was right. The truth is that this never-ending insistence on having everything perfect eventually *does* become irritating and exhausting.

Cecilia was a hard-driving perfectionist who was brutal with herself and everyone around her. When she finally married, she was incessant with her demands. Her husband wasn't "emotional enough," so she dragged him to therapy; wasn't successful enough, so she made him get a better job. She didn't like the house he'd moved them to when they first got married, so she insisted first that they remodel and finally that they sell it and buy a bigger, better, and twice-as-expensive house.

Exhausted from keeping up with her perfectionistic demands, her husband had a heart attack. She then decided that he'd never been strong enough for her to be married to in the first place, and even before he was entirely recovered, she divorced him.

Perfectionism is a no-win trip. It's an endless quest for an endlessly elusive goal. Unless Perfectionists can come back to earth and settle for real life, with all its imperfect and provisional solutions, they will wear themselves out and everyone else with them.

What's Really Going On?

Most perfectionists have grown up in the midst of one perfectionist and one out-of-control parent—for example, a drug or sex addict, an alcoholic, an hysteric, a gambler, or a manic depressive. As a consequence of the behavior of the chaotic parent, their childhood world was out of control, and, following the example of their perfectionist parent, they decide that their task is to try to perfect at least some part of it. But of course because this is impossible, they're ultimately doomed to failure. *Their emotional wound is a profound lack of safety,* and they cope with this by becoming hyper-responsible.

One of eight children, Ruth had grown up in chaos with a mother who always talked about the perfection of heaven—life after death—and a father who was a raving alcoholic. Her mother taught Ruth by example that no problem was insurmountable. She was constantly cleaning up after the messes that Ruth's father made, always covering up for him when he was too hung-over to go to work, keeping the children quiet when he was drunk, and trying to keep the house as orderly as possible so he wouldn't have anything to complain about (which was hard to do with all the kids running around).

Ruth helped as much as she could but determined that she didn't want to wait for death for life to start being beautiful; she left home at sixteen. She went out and got a job and an apartment of her own, which she painted pink and decorated like something out of *House Beautiful.* Living alone, she reveled in her ability to keep everything perfectly in place, as well as the blissful quiet after living in her family of ten. Due to her meticulous attention to detail, she became a successful secretary, rising in position to assist men higher and higher on the corporate ladder of a prominent electronics corporation. Eventually a high-level manager fell in love with her and they were married.

Her success in improving her lot in life inspired her to believe that the sky was the limit. She was overjoyed, therefore, when her son Roy was born and decided that he would be the "perfect" son. She made him a perfect room in their perfect house and waited for him to grow up and be perfect.

As time went on, however, two things emerged: Roy, who shared his father's interest in electronics, created a lot of clutter and imperfection in his room, and this drove Ruth crazy. She was always coming into his room, straightening out his drawers, and telling him how everything ought to be arranged. Her husband also turned out to be not quite perfect. Although he really never drank to excess, he would have a glass or two of wine on a few rare business occasions. This of course was unacceptable to Ruth, who couldn't resist heavy-handedly harping on him. Eventually she ended up alienating both her husband and son so completely that her son no longer speaks to her and, after eighteen years of trying to please her, her husband left her.

Not all Perfectionists have even one Perfectionistic parent. Indeed, many Perfectionists are themselves forced into playing the role of parent at far too early an age. This becomes necessary when through death, divorce, workaholism, mental illness, or addiction a functioning parent is missing, and so the budding Perfectionist steps in to take that parent's place. In some instances, they also take on the role of being an emotional spouse to the remaining parent. It may be that this parent prefers them to their actual spouse or because the spouse is missing. Whatever the specifics, these children, sensing the gap, and believing they should be able to fill it, take on an adult role far too early.

For example, Ann's father died when she was five. Her high-strung mother was devastated and, incapable of taking care of herself, she leaned on little Ann, asking her advice on every decision. While of course she wasn't actually capable of the role, Ann tried valiantly to be her mother's advisor, companion, and mate, becoming such a Perfectionist that in adulthood she can't hold a job because she's too afraid of making a mistake.

Similarly, Katy became a "parent" to her younger brother and sister because her mother was an alcoholic and her father was a country doctor who rarely came home until long after dinner and bedtime for both of her siblings. While he was out doing his work in the world, Katy was doing his work at home, looking after his wife and young children.

No matter what their particular family configuration, Perfectionists' endeavors are a way of compensating for the family dynamics that made them feel as if their world was out of control. Because they saw what was going on, they felt responsible for bringing it under control. It is this feeling of being responsible against all odds that is every Perfectionist's burden.

Since children may reasonably expect their parents to provide them with a predictable and orderly world, when this does not happen, the child's only way of understanding what's going on is to believe that it's somehow *their* fault and that they have to correct it. They do this because facing the fact that their world actually is in some way out of control—their mother *does* go into unpredictable rages, their father *does* go on benders for days upon end—is unbearably frightening.

At bottom, Perfectionists suffer from a profound sense of a lack of safety, and they try to shore up their foundering, chaotic worlds with the sturdiness of their efforts. As a result, they are hyper-responsible. Like a person suffering from Post-Traumatic Stress Disorder, Perfectionists can never let down their guard, because they believe that if they're not paying attention at all times to the circumstances of their own lives and those of everyone around them, all hell will break loose. They wear themselves out trying to cover the bases of all the things that could possibly go wrong.

Kevin, the oldest of five children, the rest of whom were girls, took on this burden early. Kevin's father, a traveling salesman, was always gone, and, as Kevin later found out, having a series of affairs at all his stops along the road. Kevin was left with his mother to manage the house—and the girls. He worried about them constantly. Every time he went out with one or more of his sisters, he'd worry, checking to see if their bicycle wheels were loose, or if the tree branch that had fallen in the front yard was at just the level that could scrape their eyes, or if one of them had left their skates out in the driveway, which the rest of them might trip on.

Now, as an adult, he's the same way with the women he dates, ever on the alert, protecting them from stepping in puddles, rolling up the windows of the car so they don't get a chill or opening them a crack to make sure they get just the right amount of breeze, reminding them to bring a jacket, helping them over the curb. Although most of his lovers appreciate his attention to detail, he says that some have found it tedious. As for himself, he admits he's so exhausted from paying attention to all these things that he frequently just collapses and has to take a time-out from his relationships.

The Difference Between a Perfectionist and Everyone Else

The difference between Perfectionists and the rest of us is that Perfectionists can never ever be satisfied and the rest of us can be—at least some of the time. Most of us, in spite of certain disappointments, noticeable limitations, or imperfections *will* generally be satisfied with an imperfect relationship because underneath it all we know that no relationship is perfect. Or, we'll be satisfied with life and its many imperfections because we know that this is the way it is.

Perfectionism often generalizes. That is, a person who is a Perfectionist in one area may seek perfection in other areas of life as well, whether or not he or she is highly developed in that particular area. For example, the person who likes her drawers arranged perfectly will also unconsciously hope for the perfect relationship, the perfect house, the perfect job, the perfect array of friendships, and the perfect vacation. And since Perfectionists generalize, they are often disappointed not only in those areas of life where they have enough talent to reasonably assume they can achieve something close to perfection, but also in all the areas where they can't possibly obtain it.

The rest of us settle for provisionality in every aspect of life. That is, we know that in every area of life there's a certain point where this is as good as it gets—it's a good enough relationship, a good enough apartment, a good enough vacation. And when it comes to relationships, we know that someone is a good enough lover, sweetheart, friend, or child to win our love and make it enjoyable enough for us to pass the time with them.

What Perfectionists Have to Teach Us

Perfectionists make the world better in all the avenues in which their perfectionism expresses itself. They make the world beautiful and strong. They give us a vision of "how it could be."

That's because Perfectionists are the Platonists of the relationship types. That is, they try to bring everything up to the level of an invisible ideal. They remind us that the situation *could* always be better, more elegant, more perfectly timed, tidier, more under control, better organized, more efficient, more beautiful than we've envisioned it or arranged it at the moment. They insist that they themselves could be stronger, more kind, more emotionally honest, more spiritually aware.

Through their control and judgment, their constant seeking of perfection, they hold us in an awareness that somewhere out there there is an ideal that we're all striving for. Most of us have lost sight of the ideal, and a lot of us have given up on even making an effort toward it. But Perfection-ists, with their conviction that perfection can and should be obtained (and the willpower to go with it) remind us that, as a matter of fact, things could be a whole lot better than they are.

What Perfectionists Need to Learn About Relationships

Perfectionists need to learn that all people are flawed—and that includes the Perfectionist. No matter how hard you try, no matter how perfectly the napkins are folded, the camping equipment is stowed, or the situation has been analyzed, other people cannot be perfectly perfected. They can improve. They can change some if they want to, but they'll generally do what they want, when they want to, and you're only responsible for yourself.

The more you can rest in the awareness that things are all right just as they are, the more you can see that there's more to a relationship than just having it in order, and the more you will be able to enjoy it. Instead of its being a project, another raft of responsibilities, a relationship can be a place where you can find rest. By making yourself available to more experiences that you are not in charge of, you can discover the pleasures of spontaneity, the joys of irresponsibility, the random, happy offbeat events that catch you by surprise.

Perfectionists also need to remember that in any relationship *some* things will be just perfect, a number of things will be imperfect or mediocre, and a few things will be downright lousy. This is an average appropriate mix for any *good* relationship.

What Perfectionists Can Do to Come Into Balance

1 Loosen your standards.

To practice becoming more accepting of the imperfections of life, you need to do two things. First, you need to try to be a bit more accepting of the person you're relating to (and anyone else who might show up in your circle as a potential sweetheart or lover). When things come up that show you your partner isn't perfect, that the date isn't going to be perfect—she's twenty minutes late, he didn't bring flowers, she forgot to pick up the dry cleaning—say to yourself, "Everyone's entitled to make a mistake."

Perfectionists have a tendency to generalize from one tiny thing—the lost laundry—to overall chaos. It feels like if you let them get away with forgetting the one shirt that wasn't picked up from the cleaners, you're on a slippery slope that will land you back in childhood and they'll be drunk, dancing on the table in their underwear, threatening to hit you. By saying to yourself (every time), "Everyone's entitled to make a mistake," you cut off the generalizing process and stay in the present moment with the specific little problem.

Also, because Perfectionists have such a great need to be in control, it's helpful to allow your partner to be in charge some of the time. Let him take you on a picnic, plan the weekend away, surprise you with a spontaneous lovemaking session. The more you relinquish control, the easier it will be and the more you'll see that there are other aspects to a relationship besides masterminding a plan to resolve all its imperfections.

2 Focus on the good things about the person you're relating to by expressing your appreciation.

We can't be in two places at the same time. You can't be loving and judging simultaneously. To move toward being accepting of the way the other person is and to expand your capacity for love, try expressing your appreciation. Everybody on Earth has something you can appreciate them for. Instead of beginning with the half-empty glass or what isn't right about Susie-Q, start by taking note of what is right and then express it out loud.

What we hear ourselves say is what we begin to believe, and the more we hear ourselves say it, the more strongly we believe it. It's easy for a Perfectionist to express resentment: "You didn't do . . ." "You never will . . ." "You don't . . ." "Why can't you. . . ." But it's precisely when you're expressing your resentments that your appreciations will also become, by contrast, most clearly visible to you. In fact, it's a natural psychological phenomenon that appreciations always follow resentments. Once you complain about how Susie is always late for your dates, you suddenly remember how beautiful she always looks when she arrives. Instead of being focused on her imperfections, you suddenly see how lucky you are that she's there at all.

So, there are two parts to this exercise. The first is, when you notice yourself expressing a resentment, follow it immediately by expressing an appreciation. For example, "You're so hypersensitive, I hate to be around you; I'm always afraid I'll put you in tears. . . . On the other hand, it was really beautiful to see how touched you were by Ryan and Cheryl's wedding. I wish I could be as emotionally alive as you are."

Second, pay the person compliments. As you do you'll hear yourself saying out loud why it is that you're with them. "You're so funny. Your phone messages are a crack-up." "You're a wonderful lover." "I love talking to you. You always have a surprising new angle to contribute." "You're so calm. When you're around I feel as if everything is going to be all right."

3 Practice gratitude.

As an exercise to get you over perfectionism, at the end of each day make a list of all the things you're grateful for. Most Perfectionists come to the end of each day with a sense of what didn't go right—what they didn't do right, what their employees didn't do right, how they didn't handle a certain situation perfectly or, in even more instances, how their boss, wife, or child didn't handle a situation perfectly—or, in a grand slam, what isn't right with the world. They also have lists of the tasks they've got to do tomorrow.

All these things leave you with a negative feeling. If you end the day by expressing your appreciation, on the other hand, you will see that whether or not everything was perfect, certainly a lot of things were good enough. They were, perhaps, even wonderful. By noticing them you will go easier on yourself and those around you.

4 Cultivate a spiritual practice.

The Perfectionist's insecurity comes from living in the psychological bind of believing that they have to be in charge, while at the same time knowing deep down that they can't make everything perfect. Only God can do this, and that's why, sooner or later, you need to turn this responsibility over to a force that is greater than yourself. Whether you call this God, the divine, a higher power, the Force, or the Plan, you will find more and more ease as you surrender to it.

It's often hard for Perfectionists to believe in a higher power because in childhood their experience was of a world that was out of control; God—if he or she existed—seemed nowhere in sight. In addition, because they've been so responsible for so long and, usually starting at such an inappropriate age, Perfectionists are now addicted to responsibility. Like all other addicts, they need to give up their drug—responsibility—and surrender to something greater than themselves.

If you don't believe in God and even the concept of a higher power is difficult for you to entertain, you can still begin your spiritual practice by consistently putting yourself in some situation where you feel beauty or awe. Perhaps for you that's being in nature, standing in the presence of a mountain that's been there for eons, or walking along the shore of the ever-moving ocean. Hiking or surfing, you may see God. Or you may be drawn to a sense of that power beyond yourself by offering yourself in service—volunteering at a hospice, for example, where you can observe the mysteries of death, or in a hospital, where you can be touched by the miracles of healing. If these things don't attract you, you may want to begin by doing a simple spiritual practice such as meditating or chanting. These practices can actually change the way your nervous system functions, bringing you, over time, a greater feeling of inner peace.

Above all, Perfectionists need to bow to the simple truth that in life there are no guarantees—no matter how much you wish there were—and to recognize that you yourself cannot create safety. On the other hand, you also need to remember that life generally isn't as chaotic as you fear. There's a safety beyond the safety that we ourselves can provide. But you will only discover this when you turn your life over to a force that is greater than yourself.

A Meditation for Perfectionists

Okay, I give up. I'm ready to stop running the entire world. I'd like a rest. Please (please please) help me stop being responsible for everything. Please help me relax and be happy with life as it is. And, by the way, thanks for all the wonderful love and relationships I have.

Balancing Affirmations

Nobody's perfect.
It's okay to make mistakes.
It's not all up to me.
Somebody else is in charge.
I'm safe.

7

THE FANTASIZER

"It'll be better when . . ."

FANTASIZERS ARE THE SWEET-NATURED ROMANTICS of the love types. They believe in magical interludes, starcrossed lovers, beautiful futures, and impossible dreams. They believe in the pot of gold at the end of the rainbow, the happy endings of Hollywood movies—and with their romantic enthusiasm they make the rest of us almost believe in these things too.

Hope springs eternal in the Fantasizer's breast as they weave beautiful pictures of the best possible outcomes. They're a delight to be around because they're always about to strike it rich, go off on a wonderful adventure, be discovered as the fabulous photographer they are, or find the girl of their dreams. They haven't just met a man, they've met the

151

most handsome, attractive man. They didn't just have dinner, they had the most romantic candlelit dinner.

Like Emoters, they tend to exaggeration, but are much lower keyed about it. They don't need to blast you with their feelings, but emotional scenarios are at the heart of their worldviews. They always believe that their situation is about to change—for the better. It will be better when . . . he finishes college . . . she quits drinking . . . we take that European vacation . . . you get your inheritance.

Fantasizers look at the world through rose-colored glasses, which makes them good salespeople and promoters of themselves and others. Fabulous dreamers, they may have trouble knuckling down to take the specific steps necessary to accomplish their heart's desires.

For example, Judy, in her early forties when I met her, was going through divorce number four. Somehow none of her relationships had quite worked out, but she knew that Mr. Right was out there somewhere, just waiting to cross paths with her. All she had to do was meet him.

In the six years I knew her, she *did* meet him—over and over again. Every new man she went out with would seem just perfect when they first started dating. But then somehow, after a while, it wouldn't work out and she'd be thrown back into the dating scene once again. Despite her many aborted romances, I never saw her discouraged or depressed.

That same spirit of optimism and enthusiasm permeated everything she did. Employed as a cleaning lady, she just knew she could create a wonderful, more meaningful job for herself—and, like Mr. Perfect, it was always just around the corner. One day she was meeting people who would set her up in an antique business; the next she was about to open her own high-fashion boutique with money from foreign investors. When that didn't work out, she tried real estate, where in no time she would make a million bucks. Nothing ever panned out, but she never stopped dreaming and scheming, convinced that any day now it would happen.

Telltale Signs of a Fantasizer

- You often live in the future.

- You write scenarios about "how it's going to be."

- People have to "call you back to reality" or tell you that "it isn't the way you think it is."

- You are a "romantic."

- You have trouble getting mad.

- You don't believe the facts other people report about the relationship you're in.

- You are often emotionally crushed when a relationship ends.

A Closer Look: Distinguishing Characteristics of Fantasizers

1 The Fantasizer lives in the future.

Fantasizers live in a time-distorted world because, rather than sipping the nectar of the present, they're always imagining a glossy, rosy future. They can never quite settle down and be in the present. They're always wondering, watching, waiting, and imagining what will happen next in the foreseeable or only imaginable future, when "life will be perfect," all their problems will be solved, and all their dreams will come true. Well, maybe not all their dreams, but at least the specific dream or scenario that they're fantasizing about right now. It may be about the gorgeous girl who just showed up in their office, or the TV star they got a glimpse of at the car-wash yesterday. It's definitely not about a meat-and-potatoes kind of guy or a girl-next-door type who's standing right next to them and could offer them a real relationship. Whatever is actually going on, the Fantasizer ignores the experience of the moment and keeps dreaming of the future.

2 They disregard facts.

One way or another, the Fantasizer isn't in touch with things as they are and refuses to take a hard look at reality. Like the credit card addict who doesn't face that the 18 percent interest that he's paying on his $5,000 debt is going to add up to $30,000 over the next several years, so the relationship Fantasizer disregards the facts that are staring him in the face.

On an extended European vacation, Phil had a brief affair in Copenhagen with a beautiful young model named Inga. He was there just for the weekend, met her outside Tivoli, and they spent two glorious nights making love and doing the town. When he left the following Tuesday, they exchanged phone numbers and addresses, and, as he continued his travels he sent her postcards from all the cities he visited.

A month later when he got home he started calling her. In one of their earliest conversations, Inga allowed as how the distance between them made them, as she called it in Danish, "geographically undesirable" to one another. Not hearing her reality-based remarks, Phil continued to call her from time to time, fantasizing that one day he'd go back to Copenhagen and they'd take up where they left off.

Three years later he did go back to Denmark. Ringing her up on the phone he discovered that in the intervening time she had been briefly married and now had a two-year-old son. Once again he courted her, but this time, being a single young mother, she refused his advances, saying that she didn't feel it was appropriate that they continue their relationship.

Somewhat dejected, Phil continued his travels and once again returned home. A few months later, he called her to "see how she was doing." This pattern continued until, seven years after their original meeting, he once again returned to Copenhagen. Although she was still divorced, her young son was now five and she was happily dating a Danish businessman. Joining her for tea one afternoon, Phil lamented, "But I came back because you're the woman I always expected to marry."

Wondering about her own part in this, Inga was frankly aghast that for seven years he had been holding this fantasy while she had herself married, divorced, become a mother, pursued her own life's work, and had a series of relationships. It took an almost-screaming fight in a public café for her to convince him that he had spent the seven years in a delusion based on a brief, albeit enjoyable, romantic interlude. Phil went home crushed, lamenting to all his friends about how the woman he loved had rejected him, while all of them had been telling him for years to give it up—it was only one of those travel affairs that people have from time to time.

In a similar vein, Jenny, a lesbian who had been consciously aware of her sexual orientation since the age of three, fell in love with Linda, a recently divorced mother of two who had never before been in a gay relationship. They had a brief and enjoyable sexual affair, after which Linda announced that, while it had been an important and life-changing experience for her, she was really heterosexual.

Undaunted, Jenny continued to court her, showering her with gifts and flowers, endearing herself to Linda's children in spite of the fact that Linda was now deeply involved with a man whom she openly stated she was contemplating marrying. This unrealistic scenario—with Jenny in hot pursuit and her former lover consistently withdrawing—went on for almost a year and concluded only when, heartbroken by the news, Jenny learned of her former lover's wedding.

A similar fate was true for John, who, having been in a number of gay relationships, kept trying to pretend that he was straight. He dated a number of women, became engaged, and eventually even married, telling himself that at any minute his attraction for men would subside. He and Lucy, his wife, would have kids and the heterosexuality that seemed to have eluded him for years would finally descend and lock him into the marriage orbit.

Of course this never happened. It was only when Lucy was so frustrated by his inconsistent sexual behavior and had an affair herself that he finally faced the music and had the courage to acknowledge that he was gay. Not long after, John and Lucy ended their marriage by mutual agreement.

Another form of not living in reality that Fantasizers routinely engage in is having relationships with lovers so many years older or younger that, realistically, these connections will never fulfill themselves in a long-term, happy relationship. For a mutually satisfying two years, Paula had an affair with a man twenty-seven years younger than she, then fell apart and became almost suicidal when, after talking openly about it, he left her for a woman closer to his own age. "But I always thought we'd get married," she said at the height of her unrealism. Her young lover, who had also enjoyed their association, said, "I know we had a great connection, but how could you ever have *possibly* imagined that we would get married? It simply isn't realistic."

For the Fantasizer, this unrealism can take the form of saying such things as, "Of course he'll adopt my six children." "Of course we'll start out by going on a month-long exotic vacation." "I met him at a weekend conference. I could tell by that look in his eyes that he was in love with me. No matter that he was married or that when we said good-bye he insisted he was staying with his wife. I just know that when he gets home, he'll leave her."

The fascinating thing about all these statements, of course, is that they do each have some basis in fact. *There are exceptions to the rule:* people have met their true love on a European vacation, have changed their sexual orientation, have had long-lasting relationships with an age discrepancy of twenty or thirty or more years (Fred Astaire and his wife; Gene Kelly and his; Earl Warren, chief Justice of the United States and former governor of California, and his wife; Mary Tyler Moore and her husband, to name a few), or have left their wives for their mistresses. But that's what they are— exceptions. To the Fantasizer, however, the exception is the rule and it's always just about to happen to them.

3 The Fantasizer has a program.

Rather than looking at present time or the reality of the situation, the Fantasizer is going to change the way things are—and most often that's by changing the way you are: "I'll get him to stop drinking." "I'll get him to stop smoking pot." Or, "Even though she swears she doesn't want to have children, I'll get her to come around." "It's weird that we never make love, but after we get married he'll be a better lover." "I know he had all those relationships with men, but I'm the woman who can turn the tide." "He's not demonstrative and he's really frighteningly quiet in company, but after we get married, he'll learn to talk." "He never brings me flowers but I know I can train him to."

These wild expectations actually represent a program that the Fantasizer is sure that he or she can implement. As anyone other than a Fantasizer has learned the hard way, it is virtually impossible to change anyone else—particularly if they don't want to change. Such presumption demonstrates once again the Fantasizer's lack of contact with reality.

4 The Fantasizer is easily and frequently crushed.

The Fantasizer isn't living in reality, and since reality is, in fact, where sooner or later we all have to live, the Fantasizer is frequently caught up short when reality nips at his or her heels, or more likely, chews off their leg like a wild dog on the loose. Rather than coming to terms with reality and "getting it"—"I can see now I wasn't being realistic; twenty-six years *is* too big an age difference. I guess it's not surprising that he left me." Or, "No, a seven-year intercontinental telephone romance will not lead to marriage," the Fantasizer is devastated and shocked when reality bongs him on the head like a coconut falling from a tree.

Fantasizers don't get it that there's more to reality than their particular Kodak photo frame of it. They're always imagining that their view of things is how it's going to be, and are emotionally devastated when it doesn't turn out that way. Usually, however, their devastation lasts only until they cook up their next fantasy, and then they're off and running again.

5 Fantasizers use their fantasies to avoid hard work.

I once knew a man who was a quite talented artist, but found it difficult to market and promote himself. Instead, he would sit in his studio fantasizing about how a group of critics would happen onto his studio and instantly discover him. The fantasy kept him from buckling down and figuring out how to get to work and actually make his dream come true.

The same is true with Fantasizers in relationships. Like the dreamy artist who should have been organizing his supplies, making phone calls to galleries, and developing a salable portfolio, Fantasizers do everything but the work in their relationships. They have a dreamy vague picture, often from romantic movies, about what a relationship should be like—roses and kisses and moonlit nights—and are unprepared for the actual ins and outs of life as it is. They're caught up short by the need for real conversation, negotiation, compromise, or allowing for difficulties or downtime. "This is hard," they'll moan, wanting to run away from the real relationships they do have and launch into another fantasy romance.

Why We Love Fantasizers

We love to love Fantasizers because they dream the impossible dream. They lift us out of the mundane and hold out the promise that life can be extraordinary. They tell us the rules can be broken, that we can win against all odds.

They make life exciting and fun. Forget the tedious 9 to 5 routine. When the fantasizing Romantic says to you after your first dinner out, "Let's take a boat to Bermuda. Let's take a trip to Siam. Let's take a kayak to Quincy or Nyack," of course you get excited. Or, when he says, "Of course we'll live in that big house on the hill, no matter that we're both still up to our necks in college loans," you are instantly lifted out of the doldrums and fired up with excitement about your fabulous future.

Also, being romantics, they're great romancers—they'll send the four dozen roses on your birthday, find the perfect pair of pearl earrings for your anniversary, call up three times a day to tell you how much they love you. When you're loved by a Fantasizer, you don't have to worry about feeling loved. No matter how shaky your—or the actual—world may be, they will step through the limits of life as it actually is and captivate you with a vision of magic.

How They Drive Us Crazy

Fantasizers wear us out because they never believe who we are, the way things are, or what we say about ourselves. Potential lovers, mates, and spouses are turned off by Fantasizers because, like with a kite that's gone wild with the wind, we feel that we always have to bring them back to the way things really are.

They don't seem to want to live in the real world. They've always got a scheme or dream that has a toehold in reality, but whatever they're cooking up isn't really grounded in what is actually possible. Fantasizers are crazy-making because they keep talking about all the possibilities as if they were real and then look at you as if you're raining on their parade just because you won't invest your last $500 dollars in their wild idea.

Fantasizers are often careless. They will blow your last $10,000 on the diamond ring they couldn't resist buying, even though they don't have enough money for the electric bill. They'll fixate on a dream and drive it into the ground—the pyramid they're going to build, the lottery they're going to win—until you're completely worn out. And when you try to tell them that it's really not going to be possible to pack up your six-bedroom house and sail a boat around the world—at least until your three kids have finished school—they'll grind you down for being so ordinary and not having any imagination.

We also find them difficult because they don't believe what we say about ourselves: "No," we say, " I really don't want to go live in a house with an Olympic-sized swimming pool. A hot tub would be fine with me."

"Yes you do! Wouldn't it be great! Just think, we could go swimming every morning. You'd never have to go the gym again."

"But I like going to the gym, and actually I don't like swimming. Besides, I don't want to move. We just got the house remodeled. I'm happy right where we are."

Or, "No, I really don't want to get married. I've been married twice before. It didn't work out. I'd just like to live together this time."

"Oh, come on, it'll be fabulous," says the Fantasizer, thinking to himself, I just know she'll change her mind.

What's Really Going On?

Fantasizers have usually grown up in a household where someone lived in fantasy or the family itself contained a lie. Sometimes this lie or fantasy was known by the members of the family and sometimes it was hidden. But either way, although nobody talked about it, the energy of the deception could be felt as part of the "vibes" of the family or the household. *Their emotional wound is deception* and their coping technique is fantasizing.

For example, Sharon grew up in a "normal, middle-class family" where her parents seemed to be happy. They certainly cooperated with each other, and Sharon's father was a steady provider who made sure that each of his three children had all the things they needed. But Sharon's father was also a binge alcoholic. Although he never drank at home, he would go off periodically with "the guys" and after one of these outings would come home and be very verbally abusive, even brutal, to his two young sons. Sharon's mother chose to ignore this, and in front of her children always praised her husband for his providing capabilities. When her husband took the boys to task, telling them they were puny, worthless, and would never amount to anything, she would always distract herself by baking a pie or working in the garden. At the family dinner table, where the boys were often cowering, she would talk on and on about what a happy family they were.

Sharon, who was never the direct object of her father's verbal abuse, grew up in the aura of her mother's fantasy about the perfect family and kept trying to create it in her own life. As an adult she would always overlook blatant flaws in her husband, and, after her divorce, her suitors. For example, she ignored the fact that one was an alcoholic, one was a miserly pinch-penny, one told her from the outset that he wasn't really interested in her, and another was dating another woman at the same time he proposed to her. In spite of all this negative information, she fantasized that each of these relationships—any day now, next year, when the children grow up, when the guy got a better job, or after they took that vacation to Hawaii—would be perfect.

In a more obvious example of the kinds of deception that can occur, Kay grew up in a household where her mother was a long-term alcoholic, but her father never acknowledged it. Instead, he always referred to her as his "vivacious wife." Meanwhile, the three children could count on her to be on display behind a glass of bourbon starting around the time they came home from school at three o'clock every afternoon. As the evening progressed and she put dinner together in a haze, feeling happier and happier as the alcohol took hold, she would start talking about the great wardrobes she would buy, the great cruises she would take.

On certain evenings, when their father, a New York businessman, would arrive home especially late on the commuter train, she would often suggest that they get a pet monkey and dye it purple. "Wouldn't it be fun to have a monkey?" she'd say. "We could take it to the corner. We could take it to the fair and show it off. Then we'd have plenty of money and we could go wherever we want on our summer vacation."

Although the monkey idea wasn't a part of every bourbon-blotted afternoon, the proposed monkey did surface often enough that the younger, more susceptible children started imagining that one day the monkey would actually show up. Each of them in their own way had difficulty facing reality as grown ups. Kay thought she would marry a man who would be both highly successful and stay home all day to "play" with her. She did marry a highly successful attorney, but was so incensed that he wouldn't take off for months on end to take her on fancy vacations, that eventually, frustrated by her nagging and unrealism, he left her. Paul, Kay's younger brother, imagined he would marry a rich girl and never have to work. And Lila, her younger sister, married an alcoholic who she was always insisting was "about to start his own business." It wasn't until these three went through a number of years of therapy that they learned to keep their own relationship expectations within limits.

Other Fantasizers come from homes in which there's a painful lie. Chuck was sixteen when he finally found out that he was adopted. One of his father's reactions to Chuck's late-night exploits with drugs and alcohol was to finally scream at him, "I don't care anymore if you stay out every night. I don't even care if you get arrested and go to jail. You're not my real son anyway!" While Chuck had been repeatedly accused by his father of being an unrealistic fool for wanting to build his own go-cart, or Hobie Cat boat, or to travel through Europe on a motorcycle, Chuck kept pushing the limits of reality because, intuitively, he had felt the deception he was living in the midst of.

Later, his struggle in relationships was to get real. He got married, had two children, and dragged his young family off to a commune. When his wife suggested he get a "real" job, he said they could live off the land. He'd just raise vegetables—although he'd never done this before. He always veered between expecting that he could do nothing and the world would be handed to him on a platter; or thinking that if he worked really hard nothing good would ever come of it. It wasn't until, in therapy, he grieved about the deception of his adoption that he was able to find his true work as a builder-designer and bring his family together.

Mitch, another Fantasizer, grew up in a family where his parents were nuts about money. They were always buying real estate they couldn't afford, imagining they'd make a bundle, and then, when they didn't, selling at a loss. They recreated this fantasy time after time until, exhausted by her husband's financial madness, Mitch's mother left his father and, unable to create either a fantasy or a reality of her own, became ill with a raft of psychosomatic diseases and died of cancer at a relatively early age.

When it came to his own relationships, Mitch followed his parents' unrealistic example. He ricocheted from buying his girlfriends outrageously expensive presents on their first or second date (fantasizing that soon they'd be walking off into the sunset together) or expecting them to take him on expensive vacations and treat him like a king. The girls he spoiled were shocked and felt weird about accepting his inappropriate gifts, and the ones he expected to spoil him thought he was a presumptuous gold-digging jerk.

When one of his girlfriends was taking a business trip to Australia that was underwritten by her corporation, he suggested that she take him with her, going so far as to imply that she should pay for his ticket. When she explained that her trip was for business, he pressed harder. "How can you leave me at home?" he said almost angrily. "You'll miss me." "Frankly," she replied, "I don't have the $1,200 for the ticket and anyway, why did you think I would take you in the first place?" He couldn't answer, but just the same, stomped off in a huff. He'd already seen himself proposing to her in front of the opera house in Sydney and his romantic fantasizing self had no interest whatsoever in the petty limitations of reality.

Sometimes the lie a Fantasizer lives with has to do with a parent's sexuality. Willis, a Fantasizer whose father was gay but never admitted it, struggled all his life with his own homosexuality and kept trying to bring the perfect girl home to Mom and Dad. Finally, he took a leap and got engaged. By promising his fiancée beautiful things and a house in a fancy neighborhood, he thought she would overlook the fact that he wasn't really sexually attracted to her. A few months before their marriage his father suddenly died. When going through his father's things, Willis found piles of correspondence from his father's many male lovers. All his life Willis had fantasized that he could outwit himself from being gay. It was only when he discovered the truth about his father that he could finally tell his fiancée that he was gay. He is now living in reality—with a man.

Fantasizers have been fantasized upon—and at an early age. And they are mad about it! That's why *the underlying emotional issue for Fantasizers is anger.* Since the lie—whatever it was—was a secret, they couldn't express their legitimate anger about it. While they watched their parents drink themselves into oblivion, delude themselves about their finances, deceive themselves about their sexuality, or fail to tell the truth, they had to keep silent or pretend that everything was all right, just as their parents claimed.

When we're young, we expect our parents to hold the ground of living in reality. We don't see that as our job—and it isn't—and any child who discovers a lie, untruth, or a lack of realism in their parents' lives feels emotionally betrayed. We look to our parents to make the world safe for us, to know the way things are, to bring us into an appropriate relationship with life and its realities.

The natural and appropriate response to deception is anger, but children of these lies are caught in a double bind. If they express their anger, they're told there is nothing to be angry about; everything's fine. If they try to call a spade a spade, their parents simply deny it. Either way, the child can't win, and so they gradually give up on expressing their anger, or trying to call forth the truth or undo the deception. Instead, they either decide to join their parents in their fantasies—"Maybe having a monkey would be fun," "Maybe we *will* make a million dollars on the next real estate deal"—or start creating fantasies of their own: "It's not true that I'm gay. Any day now I'll snap out of it." The actual betrayals that Fantasizers experienced in childhood are the seedbed of their own inability to call a spade a spade and to live in the simple truth of how things really are. Their tragedy is that they never learned that life as it actually is can also be filled with joy.

In addition, the squashing down of their legitimate childhood anger results in a major difficulty in expressing anger in adulthood. Instead of getting angry, Fantasizers fantasize. Instead of being enraged about how the wool was pulled over their eyes or they were led down the garden path, they lay out a primrose path of their own. Not only that, but by holding steadfast to their fantasies, they make the other person in the relationship express all the anger: "No I'm not going to the moon with you, goddamn it!" says the frustrated wife. "No, you can not buy that fur coat on the credit card!" screams the over-his-eyeballs-in-debt beleaguered husband.

Healing comes when Fantasizers can contact their rage about the original mess of pottage they were sold, and then teach themselves to express even small bits of anger each time they arise.

The Difference Between a Fantasizer and Everyone Else

All of us have hopes and dreams that we want to share, but instead of living in them all by ourselves, we're willing to talk about them as opposed to holding them in secret, expecting they'll magically come to pass, or insisting that our partners walk down the road to unreality with us. You don't get caught off-guard by the dreams of a non-Fantasizer; you get to think them up and nurture them together. Instead of coming home one day and finding the Steinway piano you couldn't afford in the middle of the living room, you talk about saving for it and making it a reality when it's a dream that can be realistically fulfilled.

Fantasizers take wild leaps that can create chaos in their wake—you come home one day and find that your husband has sold the house and bought a piece of swampland to build a new house on. But you have nowhere to live in the meantime and the county is reluctant to issue a permit because the wetlands are protected. "No matter," he says, "it'll come through in time." These out-of-reality dreamers often scare the people they love or make them feel invisible because they don't consult them. Their idea is always sprung full-blown on their partners and if the partner doesn't think it's a great idea, or isn't willing to capitulate, he or she is often called a wet blanket.

In short, Fantasizers imagine that all of life should be lived fantastically. They operate as if reality can just be ignored, whereas other people understand that it's the interplay of the spontaneous and extraordinary with the ordinary in the natural patterns of life which make life and our relationships so interesting.

What Fantasizers Have to Teach Us

Fantasizers remind us to think big. They teach us that if we believe too much in limitations, the way things are or always have been, the amount of money we actually do have in the checkbook, or the "normal" and "reliable" way of doing things, we'll miss out on chances for the magical or extraordinary to actually occur. In believing they can break the rules, defy gravity, and do the impossible, Fantasizers inspire us to live the romantic, extraordinary, and out-of-reach aspects of life as well as the pragmatic, ordinary, stable realities we settle for living in most of the time. They remind us that no matter how bad the odds, we should sometimes dream the impossible dream.

In addition, although Fantasizers may be way off the mark most of the time, the times they're right on target bring us the experiences we all dream of. We did get to fly first class that one time. We did get to go to Tahiti. After twenty years, we did finally get to have the beautiful house on the hill. By dreaming, they encourage us to live our dreams, and as we do, we increase the possibility of their coming true. By refusing to live in reality, they stretch all our worlds just a little. The rest of us could go on and on, plodding and trodding along with things as they are, but these Fantasizing romantic dreamers remind us to reach for the stars.

Finally, optimism and hope are vital spiritual attitudes, and we all need to cultivate them if we are to move forward not only in our own lives but also in solving the planetary problems that we face. We need to learn to expect—indeed to dream of—the good outcome, or we'll get so paralyzed by fear and anxiety that we will take no action at all. Fantasizers remind us to hold fast to these profoundly optimistic attitudes, to nurture the vision-without-limits that can make our hearts race and our souls soar.

What Fantasizers Need to Learn About Relationships

If you're a Fantasizer, what you need to learn about relationships is that in facing the limitations of reality, you will arrive at the *real*—and remarkable—pleasures and satisfactions of a relationship. A realist knows that you can have some of what you want, but not all of what you want. What the Fantasizer needs to learn is that the real magic lies somewhere between fantasy and reality. A relationship is neither all one, nor all the other. The paradox is that fantasy flourishes when the Fantasizer is grounded in reality.

Finally, the Fantasizer needs to learn that one real love is worth a lifetime of fantasies.

What Fantasizers Can Do to Come Into Balance

1 Get into real time.

Part of the Fantasizer's problem is that they're always living in a magical future and not in the moment. Consequently they often accomplish very little. So, an exercise that's very helpful for the Fantasizer is to make a simple list. What are you going to do today? The answer isn't, "Conquer the World!" but a simple list of three or four things that you can *realistically, actually,* do today. For example, "Go to work. Go to the gym for an hour. Pick up my shirts at the cleaners. Go to bed at 9:30." The more you can be grounded in reality, the more your appropriate dreams can be separated from wild-hair fantasies, and the more some of these dreams, at least, can come true.

Second, make a list that, once again, *realistically* answers the question: What would you like to accomplish in the next two years? State some specific goals for the following areas: 1) Your work—for example, working to attain that bigger bonus; trying for a promotion to manager level (as opposed to president of the corporation); learning a computer skill;

2) Your health—losing ten pounds (as opposed to thirty); quitting smoking; starting to walk three mornings a week; 3) Your finances—saving $1,000 for a vacation at a cabin on the Great Lakes, joining the Credit Union, starting a 401(k) plan.

Next, what are your plans for the next five years? Once again, these are your plans. Where is your life going? Where are you as an individual headed? Not, "I'm going to go back to Italy and marry the girl I saw in the Piazza de Roma one Friday night," but legitimate, logistical plans for your own future. State four goals you'd like to achieve in the next five years. For example: finish building the house; start working half-time so I can write the children's book I've always wanted to write; move to a smaller house so my expenses aren't so big; go back to school and finish up my college degree.

The more you can focus on *time-oriented reality,* the more you will see that life has real pleasures to offer you in terms of realistic goals created and met. And interestingly, the more realistic you can be, the more you can *realistically* develop the fantastic or magical plans that will bring your life the color and excitement you crave. The truth is, one real fantasy actually lived is worth a hundred you can only fantasize about.

2 Ask the other person, whether that's your husband, wife, sweetheart, or lover—who they are and what they want in their lives. And *believe* what they tell you!

This is a reality check for the Fantasizer. The Fantasizer doesn't want to inquire about his date or mate because the folly of his fantasy might be revealed. If your fantasy is to have two children and the man you've just fallen in love with happens to have had a vasectomy, it might be good to check with him and find out if he's ever contemplated having it reversed. You want to go hiking in Nepal, but your girlfriend hates heights, has a fear of airplanes, and really wants to stay home and grow an organic vegetable garden. Maybe you need to give up that fantasy of climbing Mount Everest together.

Fantasizers nourish their fantasies by turning a blind eye to reality. Your partner is your reality check, and when you hear his or her input, you'll know which fantasy you can legitimately pursue. If the man you're dating says he doesn't want to have children, believe him. If the woman you love says she doesn't want to move to a cabin on the rocky outposts of Maine, take her seriously; she's not kidding. If the guy you're dating says he's been married four times and doesn't ever want to marry again, he's probably telling you the truth. If the girl of your dreams (or fantasies) says the 3,000 miles between the two of you puts you on her geographically undesirable list, get with the program. If your brother's best friend, whom you've just been out with two times, says he just wants to be friends and not your lover, painful though that may be to hear, take him at his word.

Fantasizers need to face the truth that's hard to face. Just as the lie or fantasy in their families was destructive, so will their fantasizing be in their own relationships. Fantasizers need to learn that their security will come from living in the truth.

3 Give up your savior complex.

Believe it or not, most Fantasizers have an undercurrent of a savior complex. That's because they live in a world of magical thinking. They believe they can change anyone and anything, that somehow reality will knuckle under to them; that not even the sky is the limit and that, just magically, every-thing will work out. The underside of the Fantasizer's belief that magic can happen is the unconsciously egotistical belief that they can make it happen. They don't treat it as a con-scious project the way Perfectionists do; it's more like the change will magically come to pass: "He'll be great when he stops snorting coke and I know he will." Or, "Any day now she'll stop being so hysterical, then we'll have a wonderful marriage." The more Fantasizers fantasize about life magically turning around, the more they lose their foothold in reality.

The remedy for out-of-control, inappropriate fantasizing is to come back to your own life and focus on *it*. What do *you* want? What do *you* need right now? If you want your sweetheart to walk off into the sunset with you, maybe you'd better figure out which sunset you'd like to watch and how much money you'd have to save to go see it.

Fantasizers need to learn to focus on the ever-unfolding path of their own lives and realize that step by step, just as it unfolds, life will bring its own unique pleasures and truly profound satisfactions.

4 Move from daydreaming to objectivity.

In order to make this change, do something strong and positive in your own life. Instead of imagining that you're going to find the rich woman who will support you in your career, get to work and start taking the steps you need to in order to build it yourself. Instead of imagining you'll be swept off your feet by the man who can buy you diamonds and pearls and you'll never have an unhappy moment again, make a list of the ten things that give you pleasure and satis-faction right now and start pursuing them. Do you really need diamonds and pearls, or would a new CD—or a walk on the beach—do just fine? Chances are that while you're pursuing your own interests you'll meet a real live person who shares them and can give you some real support and encouragement. You might even find a person with whom you could share them for a lifetime.

Fantasizers need to remember that a real bird in the hand is worth more than a pretend bird in an imaginary bush. Over time, a real person who reveals who they really are is more far more satisfying to know than your fantasies of who they might be.

5 Learn what anger feels like and begin to express it.

First, begin by telling yourself (over and over) that you *have* anger. Just starting to tell yourself this will allow you to begin identifying it. Second, ask yourself three or four times a day, What am I angry about? and give yourself an answer. At first this may seem absurd. Your natural inclination will be to say, "Nothing." But as you keep your attention focused on your possible anger, you'll see that there are a few little things you're angry about—the fact that your boyfriend didn't call when he said he would; that your boss made that nasty remark; that today, when you needed to sleep, the neighbors decided to tear off their old roof.

As you follow this process it will lead to the larger and more life-affecting things that you are angry about—that your dad never praised you; that your mother was so hysterical; that you never got to go to college. Awareness of what you're angry about can really change your life, because it is this anger that you're avoiding with your fantasy life.

Finally, *write down* what you're angry about. You can do this at any stage of the process—with the little teeny irritations or the gigantic life-sized disappointments. This will anchor *your right* to be angry in your consciousness, and will help you move from fantasy to reality. People who can't get angry have no way of living in reality; they can't defend themselves. The more you get in touch with your anger, the more you will be able to live in the real world.

6 Deal with the deception of your childhood.

Since, to a great extent, your own fantasizing was developed in response to a major lie or deception in your childhood, dealing with the pain of that lie will bring you into reality and open your heart to love.

Uncovering the deception is the first step. Whether you need the help of a therapist to take it, or whether you just know on your own that now it is time to face a truth you've always known but avoided, take that step now. If your parents denied your adoption, make them tell you the truth about it. If one or both of your parents was an alcoholic, face it and address the issue with them whether or not they're willing to stand in the truth of it with you. Also, join a group (Al Anon, for example) that supports your living in this truth.

Once you have faced the lie you lived with, allow yourself to go through your pain about it. This will most likely require the help of a therapist, or a wise and sensitive mate. Feel your anger, cry your tears, and then, start speaking the truth, consistently, in your own life.

A Meditation for Fantasizers

Just for today I am going to try to live in reality, to see the difference between the satisfactions of real love and my endless fantasizing. Deliver me from the unreal to the real and let me find true joy there. Let me begin to see that life, just as it is, is beautiful and good. Let me see the power of a steady movement toward my goal, and the simple pleasures and achievements of the day.

Balancing Affirmations

*Life is not a dream . . . or **my** fantasy.*

A bird in the hand is worth two in the bush.

Reality is good enough.

Goals are worth working for.

Love is real.

THE CONTROLLER

"I did it my way."

CONTROLLERS ARE THE TAKE-CHARGE PERSONALITIES of the love types. Competent and confident, they enter any situation and soon they're running the show. Often self-taught (the B.A. in art who ends up designing houses, the high school dropout who goes on to become the marketing director of a Fortune 500 company), the Controller is great at figuring out the big picture of any system, deciding the place they want to occupy in it, and doing what's needed to get there. They love to be in control of a large number of things and people, and usually have a terrible time delegating or even going on vacation—it unnerves them to be out of touch with anything.

Like the Perfectionist, in both work and relationships the Controller has strong ideas of how things should be done,

177

but the difference is that while the Perfectionist's goal is perfection (i.e., no mistakes, achieving an invisible ideal), the Controller's is being top dog. Controllers are less concerned with doing things right than with getting and staying in charge—whether that's of a $20 million project, their child's education, or what you wear and eat. As a result, they always want to be "in the know"—of office gossip, who's having lunch with whom, and, in relationships, of their partner's and children's comings and goings—who their friends are, how they're spending their time, what they're learning in school. Controllers keep a tight rein on operations at home and love to volunteer for any new job-related duties, because it gives them a chance to know even more about what's going on, and to extend the reach of their control even further.

What's fascinating about Controllers is that often it's not their penchant for managing everything that's the first thing you notice about them. Most Controllers have at least one other very prominent attribute that draws you to them—a witty personality, great looks, a calm persona, even a ditzy charm. These characteristics are so highly developed and thoroughly captivating that the people drawn to them don't realize that underneath these qualities is a desire to control that is even stronger than these other obvious qualities.

For example, Fred is a handsome, self-taught engineer who's managed to thrive in the very competitive aerospace industry through a combination of hard work, native smarts, and staying close to the people in power at his company. At home he rules the roost, quietly taking charge of his wife's wardrobe, scheduling mealtimes, and closely overseeing his three sons' education and recreation. When his wife came out wearing a red dress for a company party, he sent her back to change into a navy blue suit; when his son Joseph came home with the name of a summer camp all his friends were going to and said he'd like to attend, Fred quickly squashed the idea, saying it wasn't appropriate. One way or another, Fred has something to say about everything. And if he doesn't say it out loud, he says it by sulking until everyone gets the message that they would be better off doing things his way.

Women can be Controllers too, and while it often shows up at work, as with men, their controlling can also manifest in their relationship to domestic duties. Yvonne was a great cook and loved making dinner for her boyfriend, Chris. He enjoyed her dinners and was, in fact, so appreciative that afterward he'd always jump up from the table and offer to help with cleaning up the dishes. "No, don't bother," she'd always say abruptly, standing in his way and blocking his route to the kitchen. At this point they always had a fight. He was confused and put off since he was trying to be helpful. Finally she said to him, "I just can't stand to have you in the kitchen. You put the dishes all over the place and make a mess out of everything." What she meant was that he didn't do it exactly the same way she did.

Yvonne was a Controller. She wanted the kitchen to be just so, and she didn't want Chris to be in there. Having control was more important than having help. When he finally got it that his help wasn't necessary, he felt more relaxed about accepting the gift of her cooking. But he also began to notice that she had a lot of control issues that came out in other parts of their relationship. She had many non-negotiable demands: She wouldn't talk to him after ten o'clock at night. She'd only go out on Fridays and Saturdays; every other night she needed her beauty sleep. She didn't want him to meet her mother. She had to choose what he wore whenever they went out in public; he had to put the toilet paper roll on with the loose sheet hanging down in front. Finally Chris got so sick of Yvonne's controlling ways that he broke up with her.

Telltale Signs of a Controller

- You like to be in control.

- You're great at keeping track of everything and everyone.

- People are drawn to your take-charge attitude.

- You manipulate time and circumstances so that you can be in charge.

- You believe there's a right way to do everything—and *you* know what it is.

- You have trouble delegating.

- You are powerful and fascinated by power.

- You see all relationship issues as control issues.

- You like the excitement of the battle for control.

A Closer Look: Distinguishing Characteristics of a Controller

1 Controllers like to be in control.

It's a sheer pleasure of theirs to keep track of everything, to know what's going on where and how everything and everyone is. If the feeling of "having everything under control" isn't always a high, there is at least a sensation of pleasurable well-being for Controllers when they're in charge. They feel like a king or a queen whose kingdom is operating smoothly and they can feel proud, content, and powerful. They're on their throne and all's right with the world.

Controllers always have a way of doing something and an answer for everything. Whether their method of control is obvious or not, whatever is going on it needs to be done in the Controller's way, in their timing. They take charge of circumstances, tell you how to do whatever it is, and have a very distinct and defined way of doing something themselves. Sometimes they tell you what that is, sometimes they sulk to make it clear that you aren't doing what they want, and sometimes, if you hold your ground, they'll just go around you and do whatever they want anyway, even if the two of you already decided on doing something different. But one way or another you get it that they have a way and that you'd better do it their way.

One Controller I knew, after having a discussion with his wife about what kind of car to buy—they'd decided on a Jeep Cherokee to accommodate the kids—went out and bought the cherry-red two-seater Miata he'd wanted all along. When his wife had a fit, he explained that he'd lose so much money if he returned the car that the best thing to do would be to keep it. Like most other Controllers, whether they ignore you, take action behind your back, or have out-and-out screaming fights with you, Mr. Red Miata got his way.

3 To Controllers, nothing is seen as outside of their appropriate realm of control.

Unlike Perfectionists, who tend to focus on one area and try to perfect it—a house, a relationship, their biceps, or their own psyches—Controllers bring their "expertise" to every area of their lives, whether or not they're experts in that particular area. They always have an "opinion"—of how you should hang the lamp, what job you should take, whether or not you should wear eye shadow, how your employees should behave, why their mother-in-law should get a face lift—and somehow or other you always end up either doing what they want in spite of yourself or taking the consequences.

Trying to give herself a break from her Controller husband Rick, Jennifer decided that every night after putting the kids to bed, she would close herself in the den and give herself an hour to read. The first night she did it she "got away with it," but the second night, when Rick noticed she was absent, he drove to the video store to pick up a movie and "accidentally" bumped a car in the parking lot, causing her to have to come and pick him up. Night after night, it went on like this. Every time Jennifer tried to have some time to herself, Rick would cook up a little crisis—accidentally pounding a nail into this thumb one night, losing the car keys another. Somehow, she could never have even a single hour to herself because Rick always had to know (i.e., have control of) what she was doing.

4 Controllers tend to see all relationship issues as power struggles.

Instead of seeing a relationship as give and take, an interchange of feelings, the exchange of preferences, and a process of compromise, Controllers see every relationship issue as *who's going to win.* For months Jack had said he wanted to take Mariel on a vacation. When he finally called her up to invite her, he told her he had it all planned out. They'd leave at 4:00 A.M. on Thursday, drive in his truck eight hours to the mountains, spend the night in his tent, and then go for a six-mile hike the next morning.

Not even bothering to ask if she could be ready in time,

much less whether she wanted to go on such an adventure, he just said, "I'm really excited. Pack up your things." "But, but, but . . ." said Mariel. "I'm not sure I want to go." She wasn't sure she was physically fit enough to hike the six miles, she wasn't sure she felt safe camping in a tent overnight, she wasn't sure she wanted to ride eight hours in a truck, and she didn't know if she could get the time off from work. But this was the vacation Jack had planned; he "had it all worked out."

When she called him back later and expressed her concerns he said, "Well, I guess you don't want to go then."

"No, it isn't that I don't want to go," she said. "It's just that I'd like to talk about it because I have some concerns about my well-being and comfort." In a huff, Jack drove over to her house and said, "All right, I'm ready to listen." When she told him her various concerns, he said, "Oh I get it, *you* want to be in control of our vacation." "No," she said once again, "I don't want to be in control. I'd just like to have a say in the decision." As this example shows, for most Controllers, a relationship is nothing more than an arena in which two people are constantly vying for power. Jack couldn't understand that a desire for participation was different from a need to control. In fact, as he later admitted, the concept of sharing in a decision was something he could hardly imagine.

5 They often maintain their power through intimidation.

Sometimes this is overt—like the man who beats his wife and/or kids for not doing what he wants. But very often it's more subtle, so subtle that you aren't even aware on a conscious level that you are being intimidated. Controllers seem to exert a force that somehow gets you to do their will, as bizarre as this may sound. They get in your way, planting themselves in front of you as the immovable object that no amount of reasoning, pleading, disagreeing, tears, or even pitiful threats of your own can impinge upon. After you've been in a relationship with a Controller for awhile, you somehow just know that no matter what the situation, you can't win.

For example, Karen, an attractive brunette, had an ongoing struggle with her husband, Ken, about whether or not she could wear makeup. Ken insisted he liked her natural good looks, what he sometimes called, in subtle denigration, her "peasant good looks." While of course she could "do what she wanted"—he was subtly manipulative by putting himself in the position of being the one to confer his permission—he said she looked "more like his type of woman" without makeup. In the very way he expressed his opinion, Karen got the strong message that to go against his wishes was to court his extreme displeasure or potentially lose him to a "true peasant beauty," since this seemed to be his personal ideal.

One evening, in spite of his preferences, she decided to doll herself up to go her high school reunion—she wanted to look the way her classmates had remembered her. As they were getting out of the car, without a word, Ken took his handkerchief out of his pocket and, pretending to see a crumb on her lips, wiped all the lipstick off her mouth. Despite her endeavor to make an independent decision, at the very last minute, her husband took control.

With some Controllers, the threat that lies under the surface is, in fact, physical violence. It's simple: you do what they want because you're afraid of getting hurt. With other Controllers, the threat is abandonment—do what I want or else I'll leave you. And with still others the unspoken threat is verbal abuse—a tirade you don't have the energy to handle, arguing you into the ground, or relentlessly harping on their position until, worn down to the nubs, you finally give in.

Whether or not they express their threats directly, you always feel intimidated. And this intimidation is the invisible force that keeps you doing whatever they want you to do.

Why We Love Controllers

People are often attracted to Controllers for reasons that have nothing to do with their penchant for controlling—the fact that they're six-foot-four, funny as can be, come from a great family, have a powerful job, or own a speedboat, for example.

But at the deeper level, we love Controllers because they're willing to control everything. Many other people, particularly People Pleasers, have a hard time making decisions and figuring out what to do—where to live, what job to have, what house to buy. Controllers step in and make life easy. Do this, do that, they say, taking charge. If you're exhausted, they'll take over. If you're indecisive, they'll decide. If you don't know how to do it, they do—or if they don't, they'll soon find out. If you want to be passive and just let life unfold, don't worry, they'll unwrap it for you. If you don't know how to get to the party, they'll figure it out, and if they can't, they'll buy a map. It's a big relief to have somebody make all the decisions, decide about the vacation, plan the future, and run your whole life.

Another reason we like Controllers is that they're powerful and charismatic. They're generals and managers, in charge of things. Just being in their presence is often energizing. They're plugged into what's happening. Because control is always an issue for them, a choice between this or that in which there's always a winner and a loser, they make life seem dramatic. With Controllers, there's always a stand to take, a position to hold, a controversy to be solved, and a battle to be won. And since they're at the center of the action, being around them is always exciting.

How They Drive Us Crazy

Potential lovers, sweethearts, and mates don't like Controllers precisely because they have to be in control of everything. Sometimes, or in some areas, the rest of us would like to have a say too, and sometimes it's even fun to have a few things in our lives be out of control—something Controllers can't tolerate.

We also don't like Controllers because they scare or even terrify us. Whether or not they're aggressive and outspoken or subtle and manipulative in their controlling maneuvers, they get their message across, and we're left quivering in our boots or slinking away with our spirits broken.

Margaret, the soft-spoken mother of three young sons, was married for years to a quiet but ever-demanding controller. Over time, she became so afraid of him that, after years of sitting at the dinner table where he would systematically interrogate the boys (all of whom were too scared to give anything but the briefest reports of their schoolday), she was so terrorized that all she could do was make supper, set it out on the table, and retreat to the bedroom with a terrible stomachache.

Margaret was controlled to the point of physical illness. But another way Controllers drive us crazy is that they make us *feel* crazy. That's because they keep putting us in this invisible forcefield where we're being pressured to do something that's slightly—or entirely—against our will, but there's no way, ever, to discuss it or bring it to a mutual conclusion. "What do you mean, I *forced* you into buying the house? You know it's the only one the credit union would give us a loan for."

Controllers work above ground rearranging our lives with heavy earth-moving machinery, or underground with tweezers in our psyches, where we *just know* but could never in a million years explain it or prove that they're actually pulling one over on us. They make us doubt our perceptions; they undermine our abilities; they negate the process by which, over time, we actually could discover our own likes and dislikes and gradually develop our own strong preferences.

We also don't like Controllers, because in requiring us to live in the midst of a constant power struggle, and in a world of fear, they keep drawing us into the sense that the world is not a friendly place. We can't relax, speak our piece, hope for consensus or a compromise, and we certainly can't expect to come to a feeling of union. They give us a picture of life that is scary and unkind and of the world as a dangerous place. At their worst, as in the case of outright emotional and physical abusers, they make us wonder if God still is in his heaven and everything's right with the world.

What's Really Going On?

Paradoxically, the Controller, who appears to exert so much power in relationships, comes from a place of feeling totally powerless.

Power is one of the natural attributes of being human. Each of us has some unique form of personal power, whether that's an obvious talent, such as a gift for writing or painting, or a more subtle and difficult to identify talent such as healing or intuition. It's essential for each of us to recognize our power, because, after all, that's the gift we have to give to the world. When parents interrupt or stand in the way of a child's developing sense of power, there are dire consequences, which can be meted out for generations to come in the form of a continued pattern of controlling.

Controllers usually grow up in households where they have been overly controlled by one or both parents or where there has been a continuous battle for power. *Their emotional wound is in the area of their power,* and in psychological terms we call them "aggressive" or "passive aggressive" types.

In these children the normal process for developing personal power was somehow thwarted. The father who says to his son, "Let's play baseball," and then says, once they get out on the field, "You'll never be as good a player as I am," is impinging on the healthy development of his son's own sense of power and mastery. "You'll never make it," he's saying to his son, before the boy even has a chance to develop.

Over and over the Controller's development is somehow thwarted, undermined, or openly competed with, until, discouraged and brokenhearted in their attempt to gain a legitimate sense of their own power, these children resort to subtle and not so subtle attempts to get the only power that remains for them: having control.

Control is a second-rate form of power. It's the power you settle for when your attempt at gaining your *intrinsic* power has failed. It is expressed in one of two ways—overt aggression: "I'll beat you up if you don't do what I want," or covert, passive aggression: "I'll never be a baseball player; my father will always be better than I am. But maybe if I leave my baseball glove on the landing, I can get a little sense of my power by watching him trip down the stairs." All this operates unconsciously of course, but soon the Controller is attempting to control the people in his life through either overt or passive aggression. It's the only sense of power that he or she can get.

The need to control always represents some unfulfilled gift, some talent swept aside (by a probably also-unfulfilled parent), and this is the tragedy of the Controller. Instead of encouraging his son at sports *in spite of the fact that his own chance at sports is already over,* the controlling parent goes on to undermine the natural talent of his child.

Controllers develop because they themselves have experienced the control and abuse that they will eventually mete out. David, for example, is a Controller. His slumlord father made millions by owning substandard tenements where he sent David as a teenage boy to collect the exorbitant rents. If David, then thirteen, wasn't able to get the tenants to pay, his father beat him mercilessly. David's father had wanted to be a musician, but his dream was stymied by his own father's early death. He went into real estate to support the family. When he saw David's talent for the violin emerging at school, it was so painful to him that he denied David lessons, and instead, sent him out rent collecting.

Although David vowed that he would never strike his own children, by the time he was in his twenties, he was already regularly using his fists to exert his will on his wife and children, thus reenacting the painful cycle.

Verbal and physical abuse as well as other less dramatic forms of control naturally create feelings of anger in children. Indeed, anger is the appropriate emotional response to being overly controlled. But in a household where the controlling parent is threatening, violent, or embodies the subtle intimidating force of control, the child simply cannot express his anger. He then becomes doubly wounded—having the development of his own power frustrated, denied, or shut down, *and also* having his anger negated. Since anger is the emotion by which we protect our boundaries and teach others how to treat us well, it is essential that in the process of growing up we learn healthy ways of expressing it. Unfortunately, Controllers are unable to do this, so they express their anger about their powerlessness in the only way that they can—through aggressive or passive aggressive control.

Sometimes a Controller's feeling of powerlessness doesn't come from the ongoing intervention of parents, but from circumstances so overwhelming that the Controller's parents themselves feel totally powerless. Having nowhere to go, no resolution in sight, the parents take out their rage on their children. This is often true in circumstances of great poverty or at times of personal defeat—the loss of a job, physical injury, or debilitating illness, for example. Having lost their own power, these parents strike out at their children or, in a variety of other ways, control them. In the moment of fury, the powerless parent feels suddenly powerful; the rage that has been pent up is finally expressed, and for the moment, there is relief. This is true no matter what the form of control—whether it's verbal, psychic, or physical. That is because controlling another person in whatever way brings the physiological relief of having finally experienced some power. When this happens in a family, the child who is mistreated not only feels powerless to control the raging parent, but also, sadly, through having been controlled, learns the form of aggression that he will later express in his own life.

Because power and control are so intricately intertwined, and potentially so dangerous, any person who has been controlled and chooses to break the chain of control is giving a profound gift to himself and all those with whom he is in relationship.

The Difference Between a Controller and Everyone Else

Let's face it most of us like to have our own way and lots of us can lobby hard for what we want. The difference is that while the rest of us would prefer, say, the brown couch to the blue, we're usually willing to compromise for the sake of love or peace between people. Controllers, however, are relentless in insisting on having their own way, and will do whatever they have to, whether that's enlisting people on their side, thinking up twenty logical reasons, using psychic intuition, or just plain doing whatever it is without asking anyone else in order to get what they want.

Another tip-off as to who's a Controller is that there is no discretion in their response to situations. Whether it's where to go for dinner or where you're going to live, the Controller treats every situation as if it's a life-and-death matter, and there's going to be hell to pay (sulking and whining, if not out-and-out violence) if they don't get their way. Controllers just can't let anything slide. Nothing in their world can be out of the reach of their control.

Most of us have a number of things we like to look after, be responsible for, make decisions about, but to the Controller, the whole world is his oyster, and he will check, hour by hour, on the progress of the pearl. No matter how often you say, "Don't worry, honey, the pearl will turn out fine, just leave the poor oyster alone," the Controller just can't let go of control.

What Controllers Have to Teach Us

In general, control is good. It's what keeps the world running and all aspects of life managed well. In their positive aspect, Controllers show us the beauty of having control of our worlds. They also teach us about power. Through their use and abuse of power they show us that it is necessary to possess our own power if we are to do anything worthwhile in our lives. By example, Controllers also show us that it's important to claim our power and not let other people run us over. Indeed, in the presence of a Controller, many a person has learned to stand up for themselves or to say No and hold the line, and this is a gift whose value should never be underestimated.

Since Controllers are so good at running so many shows at once, they also teach, by example, that there's more to life than the particular little corner of the world you may be looking after at the moment. Controllers teach us how big and complex life is, that there are more levels and areas of experience operating all the time than most of us would like to imagine. They remind us that it's important to have the big picture, that there's more to life than just what's right in front of our noses, and that everything in our individual worlds is also part of a larger context.

Finally, through their use—and abuse—of power, Controllers teach us how important it is for us to get in touch with our *real* power, not the secondary, and ultimately unsatisfying power of controlling, but the power of our real gifts.

What Controllers Need to Learn About Relationships

Controllers need to see that relationships are not about control. Just as personal power offers its own intrinsic satisfactions, so do relationships. The power of love is greater than the power of control—much more fun, romantic, and satisfying than just running people around or terrorizing them with your control. Control isn't the only payoff there is. In fact, there are beautiful things that can be only be learned and received in states where we relinquish control—the ecstasy of orgasm, for example, or having a having a touching moment or a healing emotional breakdown with the one you love best.

Relationships can also be an inspiration to the development of a Controller's real personal power. The person who loves a Controller does so because at one time or another she had a glimmer of who that person really is—all controlling aside. In fact, somewhere along the line the Controller probably showed a full-face no-holds-barred profile of his real talents, his true power. The person who loves the Controller was probably deeply affected by it, and if the Controller can just stop controlling long enough, maybe the relationship can be the safe place where he can develop his talents. Controllers need to surrender to love. That's because, more than anything else in life, relationships can unleash us from the prisons—emotional and spiritual—that keep a Controller's real power from blossoming.

What Controllers Can Do to Come Into Balance

1 Start acknowledging your real power.

Paradoxically, the more you *take control* of your real power, the more your need to control will find its appropriate level. Taking conscious responsibility for discerning and using your power will allow you to sort out the things that are worth controlling and the things that are better let go of. Michelangelo didn't worry about pushing people around, he just went to the Sistine Chapel and finished his painting. Neither did Mother Teresa, she just did her work. Grounded in real power, control becomes what it ought to be—a simple, helpful, daily tool for organizing life and getting things done.

Somewhere along the way you lost—or never acquired a sense of—your real power. Do you, at this present moment, have any sense of what it is? If so, write it down. If you don't, try to go back to the place in your life where it was taken away, or the circumstances that prevented it from blossoming.

For example, a woman I know discovered this about her own power: "I think my power is with leading women. I don't know exactly the form it will take, but that's my sense.

"My journey to power has been difficult because my father always put me down for being a girl. I was a cheerleader and the Homecoming Queen, but still he always made fun of me. At home he was a Controller and insisted that we keep everything neat as a pin. He got angry at my mother for being sloppy, and it scared me so much that I always tried to do everything just the way he wanted. For years, I tried to control my house and office, keep everything neat and tidy, make sure that every paper clip was in line—I guess I was still trying to avoid his anger.

"A number of years ago, I started studying yoga. A few years later, I started teaching. It gave me a sense of having a gift to deliver; I also saw it give strength to the women I teach. I've presented several workshops which were also very empowering. I think I'd like to use my—and this is hard to say—*power*, to help other women discover theirs."

If, unlike this woman, you can't even get a sense of your power, try to go back to the most painful experience of your childhood and see if it had anything to do with how your real power was impeded: Were your instincts disregarded, your talents at gymnastics or drawing denigrated, your psychic intuitions laughed at, your intelligence ridiculed? What was beautiful about you that was denied, competed with, or attacked? That's the place to look for your true power.

2 Do something right now to develop your real power.

Where does your real power want to take you? If the power that got sidetracked is a talent for ballet, go take some ballet lessons, even if you're fifty. If your power was a knack with machines and you've spent your whole adult life being a Culligan man (as is true for one man I know), go back to school and take some classes in engineering. (The Culligan man became a late-blooming mechanical engineer.) If your gift is intuition, take a class in psychic development; if it's in painting, take an art class. Go for it! The satisfactions of controlling will never equal the rewards—no matter how late they are in coming—of using your real power.

3 Keep track of your anger.

Since your power was taken away from you, you probably have a backlog of anger. Start keeping track of it. Researchers say that we all have at least a dozen things a day that make us angry: the jerk in front of you who stops halfway in the middle of the intersection, causing you to miss the yellow light; the computer keyboard that sticks each time you try to use the space bar; the garbage man clanking the trash cans at dawn; the water heater that blows up ten minutes before you're supposed to leave on vacation.

Anger is only dangerous when we're not aware of it. That's when we start dishing it out like dinner. When you're aware of it—"I'm angry that Linda called me three times before 6:00 A.M."—you can state it simply and it will dissolve and fall away: "Linda, I'm angry that when I didn't answer the phone this morning you just kept ringing and ringing me again. I didn't need to know the movie schedule at 5:37 A.M."

To keep abreast of your anger, start asking yourself every morning—and then write it down—just what it is that you're angry about. It may be the dozen things you're angry about today, or, as you become more aware of how you were controlled, abused, or your real power waylaid, it may include a lot of anger from the past (I'm angry about the way my dad always ridiculed my term papers. I'm angry Mom never let me sing in the church choir). Keep current with your anger.

4 Notice how you're controlling in relationships, and give up one sector of control.

If you're controlling with objects or housekeeping, choose one room and let it dwindle into chaos for a month. If you're controlling with conversation—always interrupting, finishing sentences for other people, or laughing so much that you shut people down—decide that you won't interrupt for a month (and if you can't do it just by deciding, get a rubber band, put it on your wrist and snap it every time you think of opening your big mouth).

If you control by manipulation—just happening over to your girlfriend's house just as she's making dinner and sitting around until she invites you to join her—start acknowledging to yourself that you're a manipulator. Not only that, but ask your girlfriend out to dinner; you owe her one.

As you do these exercises, note what happens. Does the world come to an end because you've let go of some of your control? Does anybody love you less? What else can you do with your energy? Work out at the gym? Go visit a friend who is ill? Read a book and learn something new? Pray for peace in the world?

A Meditation for Controllers

I'd like some relief from controlling. I've done it enough. I want to have the courage to come into my real power now. I'm willing to discover how I lost it so I can claim it and use it for good in the world. And, while I'm at it, I'd like to be loved.

Balancing Affirmations

I don't have to be in charge of everything.

It's okay to let this go.

Someone else can win this round.

I've got something powerful and wonderful to do.

THE PEOPLE PLEASER

"Whatever *you* need."

PEOPLE PLEASERS ARE THE ACCOMMODATORS, path-smoothers, comfort-givers, and empathizers of the relationship wheel. Warm and caring, she's the one who volunteers to bake all the cookies for the school bake sale because she can see how busy you are. He's the faithful friend who will drive for twelve hours to see you because your time is more valuable than his. Your happiness, your well-being, is of paramount importance to them.

People Pleasers are highly sensitive emotional types. As a consequence they are incredibly empathetic, and people flock to them to receive nurturance and support, which they are experts at giving. Often they are therapists, teachers, hairdressers, bartenders—any profession in which listening to, empathizing with, or nurturing others is key. But even if they don't make their living from their people-pleasing talents, they spend a great deal of time engaged in supporting others. (One People Pleaser I know was counseled early on by her father to become a therapist, or else, he said, she'd spend her whole life giving away her talent for free.)

The People Pleaser has trouble saying No. No matter what you need or how inconvenient it might be for her, she's always willing to do it. People Pleasers would rather turn themselves into knots than say, "No, you really can't come for Thanksgiving; I've already got other plans." Accommodation is their middle name. In a disagreement, if indeed they're even willing to disagree, they're quick to see the other person's point of view and pretty easily back down

Bettina, a tall Nordic blonde, is an extraordinary beauty, who, paradoxically, has very low self-esteem. As a child, she was ignored by her parents, who, if the truth be told, preferred her older brother to her. He was strong and smart and would eventually take over the family woodworking business, which was all that really mattered to them.

Bettina was so pretty that even in grade school her classmates started withdrawing from her. The other girls were jealous, and so she was never chosen for any groups or teams. Instead, she was left on the sidelines until the last minute. This, combined with her parents' rejection, made her feel isolated and unworthy. To mend this imbalance, she became a classic People Pleaser, sharing her lunch, her allowance, even her clothes with the other girls at school, to a point where it was commonly known that she could be taken advantage of.

Even now as an adult, her beauty remains extraordinary, but she still wonders if she deserves to belong and is overly ingratiating. She's always offering to help, to do the chore, run the errand, pay for the lunch, and, uncommon for her remarkable good looks, she is extremely empathetic.

Telltale Signs of a People Pleaser

- You often put yourself down.

- You can't take a compliment or receive gifts or attention very well.

- Inside you always feel as if you're not quite good enough.

- You have trouble making decisions.

- You are always trying to improve yourself in order to get love.

- You are helpful, considerate, accommodating, and empathetic.

- The way you feel about yourself doesn't seem to match up with how other people see you.

A Closer Look: Distinguishing Characteristics of People Pleasers

1 People Pleasers suffer from low self-esteem. Inside they always feel *less than*, not good enough.

People Pleasers are so kind, warm, and generous that it's difficult for others to believe that their kindness and empathy doesn't extend to themselves. Deep down, however, they feel unworthy of love and struggle with feelings of unworthiness. People Pleasers never feel good enough to be chosen, or to pursue the person whom they imagine could make them happy. Even when they're in a relationship, they're always standing somewhere on the outskirts of it, judging their own behavior and trying to be good enough to get in.

Unbeknownst to the rest of us, the People Pleaser is constantly carrying on a withering interior monologue in which he or she never quite measures up: I'm not good enough, pretty enough, handsome enough, rich enough, smart enough. I don't have the right dress to go to the party. My hair looks terrible. I don't have enough money to take her out on a good date. I'm too fat. I'm out of shape. My thighs are disgusting. My hair is too thin, too thick, too curly, too short, too long. I don't deserve to be loved. My family wasn't good enough. My degree came from the wrong school. I'm dyslexic. My father was an alcoholic. We grew up on the wrong side of the tracks.

All these and hundreds of other big and small issues that others can hardly imagine—"I've got that ugly wart on my cheek" or "My socks have holes in them"—become the reasons why People Pleasers can't be in relationships, or, if they *are* in one, keep struggling to feel good enough to deserve the relationship they're in.

2 They have an inaccurate self-concept.

People Pleasers cannot accurately see who they are. They don't know their own value. They're not sure that, along with everyone else in the world, they have a right to be here. They often have very distorted images of their physical selves as well—imagining they're too fat, not attractive enough. As a result, they may have eating disorders or addictive patterns of another kind. The anorexic or bulimic who keeps imagining she's not thin enough, the alcoholic who drinks in order to feel powerful, or the woman who drinks to excess to feel carefree enough to be the life of the party are all People Pleasers who struggle with inner feelings of shame.

People Pleasers have inadequate egos. Unlike Attention Seekers who see themselves as the center of the universe, People Pleasers see themselves as somehow not quite worthy of being in the universe at all.

3 The People Pleaser is always striving to be good enough to get loved.

Since the underlying condition of People Pleasers is that they are struggling with feelings of unworthiness, when they're seeking a relationship or when they're in one they're always in a state of striving. Striving to keep the house clean so she'll be worthy of her husband, struggling to pay off the bills so he'll deserve his wife. Trying to lose weight so she can keep her boyfriend happy, trying to be the perfect sexual partner so the girl he loves won't leave.

We tend to think it's only women who suffer from low self-esteem, but men do too. One man told me he kept his wife on a pedestal for years, working himself into a heart attack at age forty-nine, because she was so beautiful he felt he didn't deserve her. The only way he thought he could feel worthy was by making her every dream come true. When, after all his efforts at trying to be good enough, she walked off after twenty-three years, saying she'd never been happy anyway, he faced his worst fears about his unworthiness and after her departure decided that, after all, he had been a good husband. Or as he put it later, "a too-good husband."

A young woman I know who had diabetes and was continually struggling with her health kept feeling she'd never be able to fall in love because she had a serious ongoing health problem. Rather than seeing it as something the person who loved her would accept, and indeed would want to protect her because of it, she was always trying to hide her illness and pay off her medical bills in secret. She kept telling herself that if only she could pay off that last doctor bill, then maybe she'd be able to have a relationship.

Like the woman who cleans the house before the maid comes, hoping the maid will think it clean enough that she'll be willing to work there, People Pleasers are always in a state of semi-unworthiness that causes them to strive and make effort. They never quite feel as if they belong. If the world is sweet and wonderful for others, it's because somehow they deserve it. But in their heart-of-hearts, People Pleasers feel that they don't quite measure up and that somehow they have to make up the difference between who they are and what they imagine they should be.

4 They go beyond their limits in their attempts to make other people happy and often end up sick.

Because of their feelings of unworthiness, the People Pleaser is forever trying to make everybody happy. It's as if deep down they say, "Maybe if I can make everybody else feel valuable and happy, they'll finally give me the gift making me feel valuable myself."

Always bending to the will and preferences of others, they often don't even know what their own preferences are. They are the people who are always "there" for everyone else because, sadly, they're not sure they deserve to be there for themselves. They smile and say Yes to a multitude of requests. They can't say No and give too much. As a result, they may be exhausted, in debt, or have a health problem.

Bonnie, long known for her good nature, did and did for everyone else. She carried food to people when they were sick, loaned them money when they were broke, and once even signed the rental agreement for a car for a friend who ended up having an accident and not having the money (or the insurance) to pay for the repairs. Barely crawling out of the hole of this debt, she then rented a room to a passing acquaintance who was temporarily homeless and ended up eating all her food. It was only when she fell on the sidewalk and broke her arm that Bonnie "got it." While she was looking out for everybody, no one was looking out for Bonnie— especially Bonnie herself.

5 People Pleasers can't take a compliment.

If you tell them you like their red dress, they'll say, "Oh, this old thing." If you tell them they look great today, they'll say, "You've got to be kidding; I was up half the night." If you congratulate them on their new job, they'll tell you that somebody else they know just got a bigger raise, or they'll say that it's no big deal. Their ability to receive positive information about themselves has been so deeply damaged that their internal radar isn't primed to receive anything positive.

Because we can only receive outside information that comes in at about the same level of esteem we already feel about ourselves, People Pleasers must constantly reject any praise, affirmation, or celebration that's too far above their own opinion of themselves. In effect, they have no apparatus to receive the good information that is being delivered to them. Just as a standard measuring cup can only hold eight ounces of water and not ten, self-deprecating People Pleasers can't handle the overflow of good feeling that might be sent in their direction. Their cups are already full with what isn't right, good, beautiful, or worthy about them.

6 People Pleasers have difficulty making decisions.

Because they're so sensitized to everyone else's needs, People Pleasers often have a great deal of difficulty making even the littlest decisions, or, once having made a decision, sticking to it. If it's a big decision, they'll often consult everyone they know, then follow one or another person's advice—or the consensus of all those they've polled. This doesn't necessarily result in a great decision for them, because of course the person most affected by the decision—themselves—hasn't really been consulted.

Similarly when they do make a decision for themselves, and it comes up against a request from somebody else, they often back down: "I decided to take two weeks off because I'm so exhausted, but you want me to work for you so you can go get a face peel, well. . . I'll see."

Unlike Cool Cucumbers, who just analyze the facts and then decide, People Pleasers are always caught up in a maelstrom of feelings: their own—whether they have a right to do, buy, or say this or that particular thing, given its potential effect on others; and everyone else's—how other peoples' needs will interfere with or complement their own. As a consequence, they're often paralyzed by inaction.

Why We Love People Pleasers

We love People Pleasers because they're wonderful to be around. They want to please us, and they're generally easygoing, good natured, cooperative, helpful, and willing to serve. They graciously give of their service and will accommodate to even the most difficult or confusing circumstances in order to try and help you out. They can find the perfect gift, give an amazing two-hour massage, wrap the cozy blanket around your cold feet. Being around them is like being in a warm bath of love, attention, and devotion. They will listen attentively to your problems and know just what to say to make you feel better. You can always count on them to do whatever you need, because your needs will always come ahead of theirs.

Although it's their sensitivity that created their feelings of unworthiness, it is this same highly developed sensitivity that they bring to their relationships. Unlike Emoters, they won't make a scene, scream, or put you down. Nor will they take up all the room in every relationship like an Attention Seeker. Because their sensitivity is so refined, when we're around them we become aware that there are infinite gradations of emotion that people can either feel themselves or respond to in others. It is this elaborate repertoire of feelings, which People Pleasers exhibit through their responses to others, that's such a gift to the rest of us.

They're also willing to work hard, even to do your dirty work if necessary. And when it comes to relationships, they're often so amazed to have been chosen to be loved that they tend to be generous and extremely expressive of their appreciation.

How They Drive Us Crazy

Potential lovers, spouses, and mates eventually have trouble with People Pleasers because they rain on the mutual parade of a relationship by not being able to get with the program of the good things that are going on. They can't relax and enjoy what's happening. They're often so focused on their own failures and limitations that they can't just enjoy the pleasures that are occurring in the relationship.

They're always busy reminding you that they don't really deserve what's happening, and, as a consequence, they often can't share in your enjoyment of it. In short, they're emotional wet blankets. They keep dragging you down to the level of their shame or lack of self-confidence because that's their truest sense of themselves.

Lauren was on vacation with her best friend Shirley when they both decided to go down to the hotel restaurant for dinner. When Lauren realized she didn't have a proper dress for the evening, Shirley loaned her an outfit and a few minutes later, when she realized she didn't have any shoes to go with it, Shirley offered her a pair of sexy slingback shoes. Lauren put on the shoes and they looked gorgeous, but she was so taken aback by how stunning she looked in Shirley's clothes that she couldn't handle it. Instead of saying "Thanks, Shirl, for sharing your great clothes!" she kept saying, "This dress looks better on you. I shouldn't be wearing it." Or, "I'm going to ruin your shoes; my feet are so big, I'm going to stretch them out." Because of her low self-esteem, instead of just accepting the favor of Shirley's generosity, Lauren kept harping on her inadequacies so that when it all added up, instead enjoying their meal out together, Lauren pretty much spoiled the evening.

People Pleasers tire you out with their lack of self-esteem. Sooner or later, when you turn the attention on them, you begin to see that no matter how much you reassure them that you love them, that they're beautiful, talented, or wise, they won't believe you—at least not for more than a few minutes. As much as you actually appreciate them and try to build up their self-concept, they slip back into self-deprecation and insecurity. We get tired of pouring reassurance into a seemingly bottomless pit, and, in a terrible twist of irony, their insecurity that you don't love them often ends up in making you not love them.

Although we're charmed for a while by People Pleasers' inability to make decisions, this too loses its charm over time. Sometimes, not agonizing or consulting with everybody in the world over every single little thing would be a nice alternative approach. Indecision gets exhausting over time.

What's Really Going On?

Beneath their low self-esteem, People Pleasers suffer from a deep and abiding sense of shame. *Their emotional wound is a deep sense of unworthiness.* Many of them grew up in families where they felt a sense of shame, which although unspoken, subtly permeated the household. Whether it was their parents' shame about their poverty, the unwanted pregnancy that forced their marriage, their inability to provide, or a series of circumstances beyond their control, People Pleasers "sensed" these things, and this awareness is the source of their feelings of guilt and unworthiness.

Tracy, whose parents "had to get married" because her mother was expecting her, always felt an unconscious shame about being an unwanted child. She grew up in an environment where her mother's shame about her untimely pregnancy pervaded her parents' marriage in the form of her mother's being endlessly critical of Tracy's father. Tracy always felt guilty because her mother treated her father badly, and in order to handle her guilt, always tried to do special favors for him.

Severe childhood neglect also creates People Pleasers in adulthood. When parents don't feed their children, aren't at home for them day after day when they come home from school, make them sleep in messy rotten beds, or verbally or sexually abuse them, children can't help but feel shame. This isn't just an idea. These children have had an actual experience of feeling as if they were unworthy based on the way their parents treated them.

Sometimes the feeling of unworthiness arises simply because of difficult circumstances. Russell, the youngest of a family of ten, always felt as if he shouldn't have been born because his family was always struggling. No matter how good-willed his parents were, and they were, he saw them both reach their limits time and time again—at times becoming exasperated and hysterical or having long, heavy conversations about money at the kitchen table. He felt that if only he hadn't been born, everything would have been easier. This feeling that his very existence was a problem created the feelings of shame and unworthiness that he later expressed in adulthood in the form of his overgenerosity with others and his inability to believe that anybody really liked him.

Similarly, Suzanne, forty-six, was never able to make a lasting relationship in spite of numerous suitors. Finally, she confided to Roger, a lover who really wanted to marry her, that throughout her childhood she had slept in the same bed with her sister. Her sister always wet the bed and every day Suzanne went to school smelling of urine-soaked sheets. She was often teased in school and called "Smelly Suzanne," and for the rest of her life felt so ashamed that she was afraid to stand close to people for fear that the offending smell still remained. It was only when Roger asked her point-blank why she was so resistant to marriage that she finally dredged up the "terrible secret" that had caused her feelings of shame and unworthiness.

Sometimes this inner shame is related to a problem of mental illness in the family. Elaine had a schizophrenic mother who would show up at school in weird outfits and would threaten to kill everybody on the playground. Phyllis had a schizophrenic brother who had been institutionalized for years. Every time she was asked about her family she didn't know whether to say she had a brother or to pretend he didn't exist.

Whatever the specifics, the People Pleaser, suffering from shame, has a tattered and battered self concept and is always striving to believe that he or she deserves to live, to have success in life, to have the gift of love or the blessing of a relationship. For People Pleasers, there's always the feeling of hoping yet not quite believing that somehow they can be cleansed of the shameful thing and finally be worthy of love.

The Difference Between a People Pleaser and Everyone Else

People Pleasers never quite believe in themselves. Inside or out loud, they're always finding fault with themselves, and are unable to acknowledge gifts or compliments. Other people may suffer occasionally from feeling that they are unworthy, but in general they can *appropriately* recognize specific failures or limitations in their personalities and still have a general sense of healthy self-esteem.

Instead of always wondering whether they deserve love, other people can plunk themselves right into a relationship, see where it leads and flows, and have a sense that they deserve to be in it. A People Pleaser, on the other hand, is always struggling with issues of worthiness and bringing them to the table of the relationship. "Do I really deserve this relationship?" they'll ask as a new relationship is coming toward them. Or, once in it, they'll keep wondering if they still deserve it. "Why *do* you love me?" they keep asking their mates until their mates get tired of answering.

Other people may say, "I look a little tired today," as opposed to the, "I never look good," expressed by the People Pleaser, who will also say, "I hate my hair," as opposed to, "I'm having a bad hair day." The rest of us may say, "The guy I met at that party was a lemon," while the People Pleaser will say, "I can never get the good guys."

Well-adjusted people know that they are imperfect and have limitations, but they also have an ongoing reality-based sense of their own value. They know there are good things about them that make them worth loving, and they also know that even their failures or limitations shouldn't stand in the way of their being loved.

What People Pleasers Have to Teach Us

In a phrase—that other people matter. That sometimes it's important for all of us to put aside our own needs and wants to take care of someone else's. Sometimes, self-sacrifice is important, even necessary, and People Pleasers do it with grace and a lack of complaint that is a noble example to us all.

People Pleasers are also great teachers of empathy, that emotional capacity of being able to put yourself in the other person's shoes and feel what he or she is experiencing. We could all do well to cultivate our empathy, especially if we want to have relationships that are deeply nurturing and supportive, for each of us is wounded in our own way and often all another person can do is listen and offer quiet solace.

Finally, People Pleasers teach us that some of the simple virtues—graciousness, thoughtfulness, kindness, and humility— go a long way toward making our world and our relationships more gracious. With the best of their goodness, People Pleasers create great nests for real love.

What People Pleasers Need to Learn About Relationships

People Pleasers need to understand that, more than any other human experience, a relationship can teach you how worthy, wonderful, and lovable you are. Even though you grew up feeling inwardly ashamed and somehow *less than,* love is the greatest cure for this feeling. If you're willing to take the risk and do some of the work that's outlined below, you'll find not only that you can have a relationship, but that your own feelings about yourself can change.

You need to remember that relationships aren't something to be avoided because you don't feel good enough about yourself. Rather, having a relationship is something that, when you do it, will make you feel good enough about yourself. All by yourself, with your own efforts, you may never feel worthy of a relationship. But once you take the risk of having one, you will start feeling worthy, because day by day, moment by moment, in a variety of ways, your relationship will help you develop and then reinforce your sense of your own value. When your husband keeps coming home to you; when your wife stands by you even when you lose your job; when others admire the way the two of you are together; when your children adore you—all these things will gradually lift your self-esteem until you won't have to think any more about being worthy; you can just relax and enjoy your relationship.

What People Pleasers Can Do to Come Into Balance

Since shame is the main issue with People Pleasers, they have to learn to get acquainted with themselves in a realistic way that includes acknowledging their own value, goodness, and beauty. While many of us have to learn to face our faults, this type has to learn to face their gifts and gain a sense of their own preciousness.

1 Get off it.

People Pleasers need, above all, to get off their own case. Get off the program of beating yourself up. Dump it, leave it off in the bushes somewhere at the side of the road. If you are a self-minimizing People Pleaser, you can start this process by looking realistically at your failure or "less than" categories.

If you're really honest with yourself, what is so bad about you? As we used to say to each other as kids, "Nobody's perfect!" Make a list of your failure or "less-than" categories and ask yourself if these are really so bad. Think about it a minute: Could you accept somebody else with these same limitations? For example, "I feel lousy because I'm eight pounds overweight and I can't get into my blue jeans." "I don't exercise enough." "I've had trouble deciding which car to buy; I spend way too much time deciding." "I forgot to send Sue a thank you note for the party."

After you make your list, write, in a paragraph beneath it, what you, in your People-Pleasing empathetic way, would say to the person who told you that he or she had these judgments about herself. If what you write brings tears to your eyes, you've done a good job.

2 Describe yourself *accurately* from an outsider's point of view.

If you were just meeting yourself at a party, what would you see? What would you find attractive and intriguing about yourself? What would you like best? Write this description (or, of you prefer, say it out loud) and then underneath it write (or say), "Why I'd really like to get to know the person I've just described." If this is too difficult, find someone you trust and ask that person to describe you to you.

Diane, a successful young lawyer who had put herself through law school, continually felt bad about herself because her parents had been too poor to help her with her education. She had always worked full-time and hadn't been able to get the high marks she hoped for. As a result, when she graduated she wasn't able to get a job in the law firm of her dreams and so, once again, she felt (just as she'd felt most of her life) that because of her parents' poverty, she really wasn't good enough in a whole lot of ways.

When she met Jeff at a Chamber of Commerce mixer, she was put off by his good looks, but he was intrigued by her and pursued her intently. Finally on their third date she told him how embarrassed she felt about her law school grades, and her present mediocre law firm. She concluded by saying that because of these things she felt uncomfortable about being out with Jeff, who owned his own insurance agency.

He listened attentively and then described how he had seen her. He said, "I saw an attractive woman in her thirties who seemed to me to be doing the impossible. I didn't care that your law firm wasn't the best in the state. I just knew you were a strong, successful young woman who'd had the courage to take on the challenge of that much education, whatever your grades, whoever financed your education. I even liked it that you were a little bit shy. That, in a lady lawyer, made you all the more attractive. The combination of your intelligence and your shyness made you absolutely irresistible to me."

Thanks to Jeff, Diane finally got a different picture of herself. You can too.

3 Build your self-concept.

Since People Pleasers really don't have a very good picture of who they are, and since this picture was distorted long ago in childhood, they need to rebuild their own self-concept in adulthood. Contrary to the widely held notion that you can't create your own self-esteem, you can. Self-esteem has no shelf life. You have to renew it every day.

To begin this process, buy a little notebook which you can call your Self-Concept Book. In it write all the good things you hear people say about you. Then write the date and source: "You have a beautiful smile." "You're so kind and generous." "You look great today; I love that green sweater on you." "Wow, you're really in shape. I can tell you've been working out at the gym." "You have beautiful children." "That was a great pie."

Notice how the praise stacks up, and how the more you take note of it (and let it in), the more it is forthcoming.

We develop our self-concept from what we're told and shown about ourselves by others. Even though your self-concept may be negative or undeveloped you can start right now to take note of all the good things people notice, appreciate, and celebrate about you—and build a *new* self-concept based on these things. As you do, you'll gradually begin to see that certain positive attributes emerge as being your most prominent—your intelligence or humor, your steadfastness as a friend. You'll also see that people really do value you—and that you can value yourself.

So start right now. What are the words you've heard and the experiences you've had today that show you're a valuable and worthy person? It's never too late to learn who you really are.

4 Stop doing all the things you do to try to be loved.

What are they? List them: You make the pot of coffee in the office every day when everybody is supposed to take turns; you lie for one of the guys at work because he always calls in late; you promise to do jobs you really don't have time for; you lend money you really don't have.

Whatever your area of trying to catch up, give it up. If you have more than one, and most People Pleasers do, choose one per week to stop doing. Tell the guy at work that you're not going to cover for him anymore. Tell him to buy an alarm clock. Ask one of the other employees to make the coffee, or set up a schedule where everyone takes a turn. Say NO to one of the endless requests for your time or attention. Then say NO to another one. Say NO to three in a row. If everybody always calls you on the phone to tell you all their troubles, have your phone unhooked or change your number. Or leave a different message. "I'm too busy to talk right now. I have no idea when I'll call you back."

One kind-hearted People Pleaser I know had a great big burly shoulder to cry on; he listened to everyone's troubles, including his father's and mother's. For years he had a sweet-natured inviting message on his answering machine: "Hi," it said, "just let me know why you're calling and what I can do for you." When he started the process of coming into balance, he erased it and replaced it with "This is Daniel. I can't talk to you." Not only was his tone not inviting, but in his brevity he was declaring that he was one of the people who needed his attention. He'd finally made it onto his own list.

If you're the guy who always buys the drinks, stop buying them. Cut up your credit cards. Burn your checkbook. Stop going out with people and picking up the tab. Simply stop going out. It may not be as much fun as it used to be, but you'll have more money in your pocket, and you might actually discover that you have some money for that painting class you've always wanted to take, or that trip up the coast you've put off for years.

5 Practice the art of receiving.

If somebody gives you a present, you don't have to give them a present in return. A gift, a compliment, a piece of clothing they've outgrown, a night out at the movies—instead of running out to the store to buy them something of comparable value, learn to receive what they've given you and simply say, "Thank you." "Thanks for the great black sweater. I know I'll enjoy it."

Saying "Thank you" is one of the ways we *discover* ourselves to be deserving. When you say "Thank you," it means that you have actually received, taken in, and made your own what was given. Your brain gets the message that you have gotten a gift. It takes in this information and then confirms it *to you* when you hear yourself say, "Thank you." This cycle conveys the message that you are worthy.

And by the way, start thanking the person who has decided to give you a chance at love: "Thanks for the date." "Thanks for the lovely dinner." "Thanks for choosing me to go out with." "Thanks for treating me so nicely."

I know it's hard. A young People Pleaser I know agreed as a favor to drive her boss to the airport. Knowing she was a struggling student, the boss handed her a twenty-dollar bill to express his appreciation. "No, no," Carmella said, refusing it, "I was happy to do this for you." After trying to press the money on her a second time, the boss reluctantly took back the twenty-dollar bill, folded it and put it back in his billfold.

Not more than a week later, Carmella had to do an errand for him once again. When she went out to her car, she found that she was out of gas and had only thirty-two cents in her billfold. Sheepishly she came back into the office. "By the way, would you mind," she said—and it took all the effort she could muster—"giving me that twenty dollars you tried to give me last week? Today I really need it."

If circumstances hadn't brought her to a state of outright need, she never would have come to the recognition that she deserved some compensation for her willingness to serve. Sometimes circumstances have to teach us.

6 Look at what you do for others and notice how you've projected your own needs onto them.

People Pleasers often give exactly what they wish to receive. That's because somewhere deep down inside they *do* recognize their own needs, although they haven't allowed themselves to bring them up to consciousness. That's why when they see other people's needs, they know how good the other person would feel if only their needs could be met: I know she'd like help with her flat tire because I'd sure like it if somebody could fix that rip in my pants.

Notice how you've projected your own worthiness onto others. When you look at them you know they deserve to have their dreams come true. It's as if you're saying to yourself *they* deserve to be helped; they deserve to have their needs fulfilled. *They* deserve food, attention, compliments, caring, time, generosity, emotional support. You understand because you know how sad and bad it was, how ashamed you felt inside because of not having your own needs met in childhood. But somehow, ever since then, your own needs are always left out of any equation.

In becoming aware of what you are continually doing for others, you will also, somewhat belatedly, become aware of what your own needs might be. It's around these needs precisely that you can start asking for help, attention, support, and companionship for yourself. Whatever other people need—time, listening, availability, emotional or financial support, chicken soup, or help with their work—you probably have needs in all these areas too.

To begin to remedy this, 1) Make a list of all the ways you're helping other people; 2) Then, for each category you've identified, make a second list of what you need for yourself in that particular category; 3) As you identify each of these areas, tell yourself you're going to start learning to receive in that area.

For example: you always listen patiently to everyone's problems; you always ask others, even relative strangers, how they feel; you lend money to friends in need. That means you need to be listened to—a lot; you need to be asked how you feel; and you need some relief from your own financial burdens. Remember, the way you help others is *your* cry for help.

Then, in order to learn to receive in these areas, start asking for what you need in that particular area. If it's listening, start saying, "I need to have a conversation with you. When can you talk to me?" "Can you listen to me while I tell you my troubles?" If it's money, say, "Can you loan me some money?" "I'm feeling sick, will you go to the store and get some me some orange juice?" "I'm overburdened at work; my computer's got a glitch. Could you fix my computer or help me out with some work?"

Asking will seem strange at first because your whole life has been designed around the assumption that you don't have a right to ask for anything. Start by asking for little things: "While you're up, could you get me a cup of coffee?" or, "Would you mind closing the screen door; the mosquitoes are coming in." Move on to bigger things like, "I know we made a date for Friday, but my favorite cousin is flying in from Boston and I'd really like to spend the evening with her. Can we go on Saturday night instead?"

7 Take care of yourself.

As we said before, People Pleasers run themselves into the ground. If this is the lousy inconsiderate way you (don't) look after yourself, start by setting a realistic bedtime, eating right, getting some exercise, and, above all, trying to stay aware of your own needs.

Second, what are three self-caring practices you can add immediately to your personal repertoire? Getting a massage every month? Going for a walk every morning? Turning off the phone at 8:00 P.M. so you have some time to read? Buying yourself some flowers once a week? When you start to pamper yourself, you are acknowledging your own value, and this creates the pathway by which other people can find their way to do the same.

A Meditation for People Pleasers

I'm ready to start feeling good about myself now, to stop picking on myself about every little thing, to know that I'm worthy, to rest in my value, to cherish my goodness, to open to love. I am willing to believe I'm lovable, just as I am.

Balancing Affirmations

I can be as kind to myself as I am to others.

I deserve to be loved.

I'm good enough just as I am.

10
PAIRING UP

The Love Types in Love

NOW THAT YOU'VE HAD A CHANCE TO GET ACQUAINTED with the nine love types, there's one other thing that's useful to know, and that's who tends to fall in love with whom and why. While theoretically anyone can fall in love with anyone, particular types tend to be drawn to certain other types, either because of a comfort level, or because of the possibilities for change.

In all our relationships we are trying to learn something. Because this is true, we either consciously or unconsciously pick a person whose personality type exhibits traits we need to develop in order to become more balanced. Or we choose a partner who has the potential to teach us something about the difficulties of our own type, and thus provide us with an opportunity to change. Whether or not we get the lesson

223

makes all the difference in whether we evolve and grow in our capacity to love, or simply get more and more entrenched in our old patterns.

The whole point of looking at personality types is to make us all a little more aware of what's really going on. You can live a lifetime of relationships and not evolve one iota, or, by choosing to be aware, you can see how each of your relationships has changed you. Not only that, but you can also make sure you get the benefits each type of lover has to offer, and, in the process, continually refine yourself.

Because of how difficult is it to change, many people end up just playing out their old issues over and over, but every relationship offers the possibility for you to come into greater balance. The most balanced of all the love types would be a person who's a mix of them all, representing a blend of the best of all their traits. It is this greater balance, this wholeness, which unconsciously and on the spiritual level we are all trying to move toward, whether we know it or not.

That's why, even though you may recognize how comfortable a match with one particular type may be, in your entire relationship history you may have chosen from several of the other types as well. If that's the case, congratulations! You've probably learned a lot, and your personality has been balanced a great deal.

Just as yellow and blue are two separate colors but can become an entirely new color, green, when mixed in equal proportions, so your personality too, distinct in its coloration, can be transformed by the influence of a personality of another type. Similarly, your type—yellow, if you will—can be changed in a different way through interaction with another type, and become, for example, yellow-green, yellow-orange, or even pale yellow. To one degree or another, your interaction with any other type will change you. You will take on some of their traits and qualities, and they will take on some of yours.

The bottom line is that we choose the types we do because, at any given time, that particular type has something to teach us, and because, through interacting with a person of that type, we ourselves become more balanced. Because we are always unconsciously seeking this balance, and because of the particular psychological issues represented by each of the love types, certain types are frequently drawn to certain other types, and there are a number of typical pairings.

Attention Seekers

Attention Seekers are, not surprisingly, drawn to all types who will give them attention, particularly People Pleasers, who will be nice to anyone; Perfectionists, who, seeing Attention Seekers' genuine talents, are inspired to help them bring their talents to perfection; and sometimes, if the moon is full or the chemistry is right, to Fantasizers, who lure them into their fantasies, and make them feel good. They can also, though rarely, be drawn to Skeptics, whom they can occasionally win over with their personal magnetism, but this is usually a short-lived union.

Sometimes Attention Seekers are drawn to other Attention Seekers, and these relationships often work out well—at least for a time. Each Attention Seeker is so focused on his or her own need for attention that as long as each is getting enough praise from the outside world they can coexist happily side by side, each fulfilled by outside sources. Movie star marriages, for example, are often pairings between two Attention Seekers.

At a deeper level, though often unconscious, Attention Seekers are trying to bring themselves into balance by learning how to think of other people as well as themselves. No one is a better teacher of this skill than People Pleasers, who do it all the time, which is why, for Attention Seekers, this is probably one of the most common pairings.

Attention Seekers are NOT drawn to Workaholics, who aren't there to give them any attention, or to Controllers, with whom they get into too much of a power struggle for it to be comfortable for any length of time.

Emoters

We've all seen many pairings between a fireball and a mild-mannered steady-as-you-go type and wondered what was going on. This is one of the classic pairings of all the love types—the Emoter and the Cool Cucumber. Emoters love Cool Cucumbers, because while they're blowing their stacks their partners keep cool, becoming a quiet example of how to respond (by not responding at all) in a less explosive fashion. Although they seem worlds apart (and they are)—the Cucumber is Cool and the Emoter is boiling—by mixing temperatures they arrive in the middle at a state of cozy warmth. Emoters are often frustrated by the Cucumber's lack of emotion, but overall they're grateful for it and over time they can soak up some of the Cucumber's calmness.

Emoters may also pair up with Controllers for a similar reason. In the same way that they're attracted to Cool

Cucumbers, Emoters are always looking for the personality type that will help them rein in their emotions, and Controllers fit the bill—they love to control anything, even raging feelings.

Emoters also sometimes mate with other Emoters, sometimes living an out-and-out free-for-all of emotions. This is the *Who's Afraid of Virginia Woolf*-type couple who sling it back and forth with no holds barred. While this makes for a dramatic (and exhausting) relationship, it usually doesn't last long, and nobody changes very much. It's just an indulgence in what both partners already do too well.

Emoters don't like Workaholics because they're never around to have an emotional experience with—other than yelling about how the Workaholic never comes home. This is a good temporary relationship for Emoters; they get to have a lot of outbursts. But since Emoters are really looking for a quieter and more reasonable way of expressing the emotions that are forever welling up in them, they do better with Cool Cucumbers who balance them, even though they may prefer People Pleasers who endlessly (and to both types' detriment) let Emoters indulge their feelings. This latter pairing is not progressive, because instead of creating the friction that generates change, they each just reinforce their individual patterns.

Cool Cucumbers

Basically Cool Cucumbers like best to be with other Cool Cucumbers in a serene and peaceful environment where nobody gets too upset about anything. For Cool Cucumbers who have been very emotionally wounded, this is a healing balm. These are generally steady, long-lasting relationships that are quietly satisfying to both partners, though they don't really encourage much change.

Emotion-phobic Cool Cucumbers may also be drawn to Workaholics or even Skeptics, because both of these types provide them with the semblance of a relationship without ever actually challenging them to relate emotionally to any significant degree.

Other Cucumbers, unconsciously seeking to bring their emotions toward the foreground, will choose Emoters to pair up with. That's because even though they're uncomfortable with feelings—theirs and anybody else's—deep down they know that expressing their emotions would enrich their lives immeasurably. This match is often fraught with frustration because the Cucumber, who wants to tiptoe out into the emotional waters, is often instead blasted out into them. Nevertheless, it is growthful for the Cucumber, who gradually, over time, becomes less afraid. Along with improving himself in this configuration, the Cool Cucumber, whether he admits it or not, rather enjoys the exotic explosions his partner creates. Without any effort at all, the Cucumber gets exposed to the raw energy of an emotionally vivid world.

Cool Cucumbers are not much inclined to go off with Fantasizers because they are continually rewriting the reality that down-to-earth Cucumbers rely on. Fantasizers are up in the air, scheming schemes and dreaming dreams, and when they try to corral Cucumbers into their phantasmagoria of romantic possibilities, Cucumbers just aren't interested. Cucumbers also don't like Controllers or Perfectionists because, since in their own quiet way they think they have all the answers, they don't want anyone telling them how it is or what to do.

Skeptics

Because they don't really believe in love anyway, Skeptics can be drawn to almost any type for some reason that isn't intrinsic to that type. More than likely they're attracted to a great body, a beautiful face, brains, a big bankroll, a flashy social life—anything that seems for the moment to be able to shake them out of their skepticism, and which, of course, in the long run won't be strong enough to work. Then the Skeptic uses the emotional issue of that type as the reason why, in the end, the person is unacceptable: they're too focused on themselves, they're hysterical, they're too cool to get a rise out of, they live in a fantasy world, they're too picky about everything; they're too controlling, or they just can't stand up for themselves.

Somebody has to work really hard for a relationship with a Skeptic to work. That's why they're generally not drawn to other Skeptics (between them nobody has enough fuel to get the fire started, enough juice to slake anybody's thirst), and often end up with Perfectionists (who believe that just about anything or anyone can be perfected) and People Pleasers (who are so intrinsically optimistic, empathetic, and generous that they'll pour out their goodies for anyone). It's these two types who have the best chance of helping a Skeptic break through his issues of betrayal, but only if the Skeptic is willing to do a little watering of his deep-down kernel of hope on his own.

The Workaholic

Workaholics are happy with anyone of any type who pretty much leaves them alone and gives them the basics of a relationship—a certain amount of sex, companionship, a sharing of the chores, and someone to take to the company party. Workaholics particularly like other Workaholics because nobody bothers anybody about what's not happening in their relationship. What they do for fun . . . is work. Like the pairing between the two Cool Cucumbers, nothing much changes emotionally for either partner in this dynamic, but a lot of work gets done—houses built, empires created, corporations managed, law firms established.

This is a particularly common pairing for the late twentieth century, when everybody's working too much and work is one of the highest values of our culture. These overachievers are so busy not relating to each other that they may even leave their secondary relationships—with children, houses, pets, and even their own meals—to others. Nannies, housesitters, maids, and garden and pool care services do the work of sustaining these other relationships, which is fine for the Workaholics who generally see their work more clearly than their personal relationships.

Workaholics also like Perfectionists because whatever the Workaholic isn't doing for the household or the kids, the Perfectionist partner will probably make sure that it gets done. Typical pairs of these two types can be seen in the high-powered attorney and his Perfectionist housekeeper wife, or the successful entrepreneur and his wife who is a Perfectionist mother.

Of course, Workaholics like People Pleasers too, because, as usual, People Pleasers, with their flexibility and accommodation, will fit into the busy lives of the Workaholic without complaint. Occasionally they also get hooked up with Attention Seekers, if the Attention Seeker's talent happens to coincide with their area of workaholism—the rock star and her manager husband, the actor and his director wife.

Workaholics tend to shy away from Emoters for the same reason that Cool Cucumbers do—because they don't want to experience their feelings. On the other hand, those few not quite dyed-in-the-wool Workaholics who've gotten a clue that their workaholism is a cover for something they really ought to take a look at may take the risk of joining up with an Emoter, and thereby, over time, work less and feel more. For the Workaholic this pairing can be an opportunity for real growth.

The Perfectionist

Perfectionists are happy with other Perfectionists—particularly if their areas of perfectionism are similar or complementary. Perfectionist housewives like men who are equally organized about their cars, garages, and tools, while Perfectionist dressers can be charmed by one another or by the financial record-keeping, interior decorating, or health-oriented Perfectionist. Since perfectionism is, in itself, a quality Perfectionists admire, they usually value it, no matter what form it comes in. However if one Perfectionist's area of expertise differs too much from the other's—she's a stickler about timing and he's not; he's a Perfectionist about organization and she could care less—there may be a problem, especially if one Perfectionist fiddles with or has access to the other Perfectionist's arena. One expert is likely, in his or her own perfectionistic fashion, to try to perfect the ways of the other, and thereby create an ongoing relationship problem.

Perfectionists also do well with People Pleasers, because the indecisive People Pleasers benefit from the Perfectionist's tendencies to manipulate the movement of reality and are often grateful. This gives the Perfectionist another kind of satisfaction. This can be a long-standing combination, because everybody's getting something most of the time. It also works as a teaching because Perfectionists need to learn to let go of the reins, which People Pleasers are always willing to do in behalf of other people's needs, while People Pleasers need to learn seek the goal, hold the line, and maintain a focus, the very things Perfectionists know so well how to do.

Actually, Perfectionists whose specialty is perfecting people—these sub-types believe they can perfect anybody, turn any sow's ear into a silk purse—can be happy at least for a while with practically any of the other types. That's because they can see any one of them as a project—get the Attention Seeker to be more empathetic, the Emoter to calm down, the Workaholic to slow down, et cetera. In direct opposition to Skeptics, who can chance a relationship with any of the other types—only to prove to themselves that it won't work out—Perfectionists in their perfectionistic optimism will take on almost anyone.

Once in these "fixer-upper" relationships, Perfectionists get frustrated by their partners' unwillingness or inability to change, and are offered an opportunity to learn that no matter how well-intentioned they may be, the changes they'd like to effect in other people can only originate with these people themselves. If they can make peace with this, Perfectionists can be great partners; otherwise they will be perpetually dissatisfied and eventually drive their partners away with their nagging and complaining.

The Fantasizer

Fantasizers can be in a fantasy relationship with anyone, but when it comes to having an actual relationship, it's not as easy. If their unconscious desire to get in tune with reality is strong enough, they do well with people-oriented Perfectionists, who can teach them something about the real nature of relationships; Emoters, who can blast them out of their fantasies; Cool Cucumbers, who hold a steady line with reality; and even Attention Seekers, who will prove to them time and time again that their dreams won't come true—because the Attention Seeker will take up all the airtime, and there won't be any time left over for dreaming.

Fantasizers who are less inclined to change are frequently drawn to high-profile Attention Seekers because they are captivated by the fantasy of what life could be like with these flashy movers-and-shakers. They are also attracted to People Pleasers, who will frequently indulge them in their fantasies. They also often end up with Controllers, their radical opposites, because in their fantasy life they can't believe they're being controlled as much as they are, and also because in real life they often, at least unconsciously, realize that they need to be controlled. Rarely, they pair up with Skeptics; because they can fantasize a beautiful relationship based on whatever attractive attribute the Skeptic usually has along with his or her skepticism.

Most Fantasizers, however, spend a lot of their relationship lives alone, unable to reconcile fantasy with a real-life meat-and-potatoes relationship. They have relationships with everyone in their minds, and no one in reality.

The Controller

Controllers love anyone who's willing to be pushed around, People Pleasers above all. It is also frequently Emoters who, since they often look as if they need to be controlled, present a lively challenge for a Controller. In both of these relationships, the Controller has an opportunity to learn that there are other ways of achieving their ends beside control—negotiation, consideration, compromise, and the expression of their deeper emotions, for example. These lessons are difficult, and often Controllers don't learn them because, of course, in order to do so, they'd have to give up control. However these two highly emotional types do have a great deal to teach them.

The most extreme type of Controllers—abusers—most frequently team up with the most extreme version of People Pleasers, and in this combination there is often a destructive and dangerous liaison in which both parties are confirmed in their type and no one learns anything. This is the classic combination of a battering man and a woman with low-self esteem who can't leave the relationship.

On the positive side, Controllers often choose other Controllers so they can live in an ongoing and never quite resolvable power struggle. Interestingly enough, this pairing often results in a long-lived relationship, especially when the Controllers are pretty evenly matched. While no one ever actually surrenders (which would spoil all the fun), both Controllers have an unconscious healthy respect for each other, recognizing that just as they can never get the better of their other half, he or she can never get the better of them. While these Controllers may not expand their emotional repertoire in the direction of more vulnerability, they also safeguard one another from getting—would you believe it—out of control.

Attention Seekers are also an occasional choice, but only if the Controller can exert some specific form of control in their lives, such as running their households, making their schedules, or doing PR for them.

Controllers don't usually have relationships with Skeptics because they're not any fun to control; they can see at a glance that Skeptics aren't controllable. Basically, Controllers like relationships with anyone they can intimidate—no matter what their type—and ignore strong members of any type who can stand up for themselves.

People Pleasers

People Pleasers are strongly attracted to Controllers and Perfectionists because, at their best, these strong-willed types are a healthy balance for the indecisive People Pleaser. Since People Pleasers are often rudderless folks who focus so much of their attention outside themselves, Controllers and Perfectionists have the positive effect of sort of gathering them up and setting them in a direction.

In these relationships, People Pleasers have an opportunity to learn how to develop these strengths in themselves. If they're lazy, however, they won't evolve; they'll just be dominated and controlled.

Since People Pleasers are so sensitive, accommodating, and gracious, they are receptive to all other types for any number of reasons that have nothing specifically to do with their particular type. The truth is that all People Pleasers have to do is stand still and be their pleasing, accommodating selves and other types will flock to them. As a result, they often find themselves in a relationship solely because the other person has chosen them. To consciously choose someone and then continually discover and express their own needs is the ongoing challenge for the People Pleaser, no matter what type their mate is.

A Final Word

As we've seen, every personality type represents some aspect of limitation in love, yet each of them also provides an opportunity for their partners to develop. In fact, it's often the very things about a person that drive you crazy that are the seeds of your greatest opportunity to change.

Change, transformation, coming into balance, dealing with your emotional issues and resolving them—these are the greatest gifts that any relationship can offer. In fact, on a higher level, that's why we're in relationships at all. Every relationship you choose and each partner you engage with has something to teach you. The wonderful things about each personality type are the reasons we fall in love with the people we do in the first place. Their captivating attributes draw us into the relationship where the things that drive us crazy can then challenge us to grow.

For this reason no type is better than any other, nor is any totally balanced in itself. Therein lies not only the necessity but the beauty of our relationships. For through them we can move toward wholeness, we can develop, to an even greater measure, our capacity for love.

People of every type—including your own—have suffered. Each of us carries within a wound of feeling and of spirit and we are all struggling to resolve a painful emotional issue. It is my hope that knowing this will help you to grow in compassion. As you come to understand that we all have limitations, and that every one of us has something beautiful and necessary to contribute to the relationship wheel, you will see the necessity of all the types, indeed, of every one of us.

That's why, no matter what type you are, or what type you're attracted to or are currently in a relationship with, you can expect love.

Finally, since being human is above all a journey of personal development and spiritual evolution, we are all continually in the process of learning to become better lovers and better human beings. May your new understanding of yourself and others expand not only your capacity to be loved, but also *to* love. For more love, at every level, for all of us, is truly the only thing worth living for.

A CHART OF THE LOVE TYPES

	Love Type	Emotional Wound	Coping Behavior	Unconscious Emotion that Needs to Be Addressed
1	The Attention Seeker	Lack of Love	Narcissism	Insecurity
2	The Emoter	Emotional Chaos	Hysteria	Fear
3	The Cool Cucumber	Deep Emotional Pain	Denial/Suppression	Sorrow
4	The Skeptic	Betrayal	Doubt/Cynicism	Lack of Trust
5	The Workaholic	Abandonment	Distraction/Avoidance	Grief
6	The Perfectionist	Lack of Safety	Control	Feeling Overly Responsible
7	The Fantasizer	Deception	Fantasizing	Anger
8	The Controller	Loss of Power	Aggression/Passive Aggression	Power
9	The People Pleaser	Feeling Unworthy	Accommodation	Shame

For more than twenty-five years, Daphne Rose Kingma has worked as a psychotherapist whose practice has helped hundreds of individuals and couples understand and improve their relationships.

Dubbed the "Love Doctor" by the *San Francisco Chronicle*, Daphne has appeared as a relationship expert on nationally broadcast television programs including *Oprah!*, *Sally Jessy Raphael*, and *The Leeza Gibbons Show*. A best-selling author, her previous books include *True Love, Finding True Love, Weddings from the Heart, A Garland of Love, Coming Apart,* and *The Future of Love*. She lives in Santa Barbara, California.

For information on Daphne's lectures and workshops, please write to her in care of:

Conari Press
2550 Ninth Street, Suite 101
Berkeley, CA 94710

or:

New Directions
P.O. Box 5244
Santa Barbara, CA 93150

Other Titles of Interest from Conari Press

The Courage to Be Yourself:
A Woman's Guide to Growing Beyond Emotional Dependence,
Sue Patton Thoele, $10.95, ISBN 0-943233-25-9

The Little Book of Big Questions:
200 Ways to Explore Your Spiritual Nature,
Jonathan Robinson, $8.95, ISBN 1-57324-014-1

Random Acts of Kindness,
Editors of Conari Press, $9.95, ISBN 0-943233-43-7

Stone Soup for the World:
Life-Changing Stories of Kindness and Courageous Acts of Service,
Marianne Larned, ed., $15.95, ISBN 1-57324-118-0

The Woman's Book of Soul:
Meditations for Courage, Confidence and Spirit,
Sue Patton Thoele, $16.95, ISBN 1-57324-134-2

To order Conari Titles:
Toll-Free: 800.685.9595
Fax: 510.649.7190
E-Mail: conari@conari.com